# The Truth about Padre Pio's Stigmata

## and Other Wonders of the Saint

Frank Rega

Copyright © 2012 Frank Rega

Second Edition 2014

All rights reserved.

ISBN: 1478183918
ISBN-13: 978-1478183914

# DEDICATION

To my parents Mike and Mary Rega and to my sister
Patricia Rega

# CONTENTS

|   | | |
|---|---|---|
| | Introduction | i |
| 1 | The Truth about Padre Pio's Stigmata | 1 |
| 2 | Padre Pio and the General - a Study in Bilocation | 17 |
| 3 | Padre Pio, a Patron Saint for the Unborn | 31 |
| 4 | The Pope, Padre Pio, and a Miracle | 41 |
| 5 | Padre Pio's Secret: his Shoulder Wound | 59 |
| 6 | Salvation Outside the (Visible) Church | 65 |
| 7 | The Gemma Di Giorgi Mystery | 83 |
| 8 | Padre Pio and Pope Paul VI's *Humanae Vitae* | 101 |
| 9 | Padre Pio and the Tale of the Empty Tomb | 117 |
| 10 | The Amazing Story of Giovanna Rizzani | 125 |

ACKNOWLEDGMENT

Special thanks to the many devotees of Padre Pio who have inspired me to write these articles.

The cover photo is of a statue of Padre Pio on the grounds of the Padre Pio Foundation located at 463 Main Street, Cromwell Ct. (www.padrepio.com).

# INTRODUCTION

This is a collection of articles on Padre Pio, many of which have been previously published in Catholic periodicals. Those published here for the first time are chapter 7, "The Gemma Di Georgi Mystery," chapter 8, "St. Padre Pio and Pope Paul VI's *Humanae Vitae*," and chapter 10, "The Amazing Story of Giovanna Rizzani."

A major reason for collecting these articles in a more permanent fashion is to safeguard what is written in the first chapter, "The Truth about Padre Pio's Stigmata." This essay was specifically composed to refute the false allegations that the stigmata of the Padre were created or maintained by artificial means, such as chemicals.

All translations from Italian language sources are by the present author. Online articles can be found by doing an Internet search on the title. Internet articles that have been removed from the web might have been archived online by the site www.archive.org.

"The time best spent is that which is spent for the glory of God and the salvation of souls."

"Pray, hope and don't worry. Anxiety doesn't help at all. Our Merciful Lord will listen to your prayer."

"Prayer is the best weapon we possess, the key that opens the heart of God."

"Often kiss Jesus with affection and you will recompense Him for the sacrilegious kiss of the unfaithful Apostle, Judas."

"The Cross is the standard of the elect. Let us always keep close to it and we will succeed in conquering in everything and over everyone."

**Padre Pio**

# Chapter One

## The Truth about Padre Pio's Stigmata
*Answering the carbolic acid accusations*

When Canada's McGill University conferred its $75,000 "Cundill Prize in History" to a book about Padre Pio,[1] the *Montreal Gazette* reported on Nov. 15, 2011 that the book raised the possibility that the saint used carbolic acid to self-inflict the wounds of his stigmata.[2] The carbolic acid canard was quickly seized by the press. The next day *The Telegraph* of Britain announced that "Italy's Padre Pio used carbolic acid to cause bleeding wounds on his hands that he claimed were replicas of Christ's, according to a new book." [3] The Huffington Post reported that the book suggests that "Italian saint Padre Pio reportedly used carbolic acid on his hands, feet and sides to 'self-inflict' the wounds…" [4]

A large spate of articles soon followed both in print and online, which cast doubt upon the authenticity of Padre Pio's stigmata. Even Catholic websites parroted the claim. The faith of many Catholics in the canonization process as well as in the sanctity of Padre Pio was shaken.

Of course it was also convenient fodder for opponents of the traditional Church, especially critics of her veneration of the saints.[5] Concerned about possible distortions, British editor and columnist Damian Thompson wrote: "What bothers me about the claims about Pio – which I haven't studied closely enough to evaluate – is that they will be used by the secular world and its Catholic allies to pour scorn on the peasant and working-class devotions that Vatican II ideologues tried to eradicate." [6]

However, the charge that St. Padre Pio used chemicals to sustain the stigmata was shown to be baseless as far back as 1919, less than a year after their occurrence. In that year, a little-known attempt at a medical "cure" effectively ruled out chemical agents as the cause of the wounds on the saint's hands, feet and chest.

Only three official medical examinations of St. Pio's wounds were ever authorized, and they all occurred in 1919. The examining physicians did their work independently of the others. One of the three was Dr. Amico Bignami, Professor of Pathology at the Royal University of Rome (Regia Università di Roma). Dr. Bignami was invited to the friary at San Giovanni Rotondo by the Procurator

General of the Capuchin Order, in response to a request from the Holy Office at the Vatican. He was asked to perform a medical examination on the wounds of Padre Pio, and to render his judgment. [7]

Bignami was an atheist and logical positivist, which meant that he would only give credence to phenomena which could be proven scientifically or explained naturally. At first he refused the commission, but upon learning that the request originated from the Curia, he accepted, but wished no one to know of the assignment. [8]

## The Examination

He arrived in July of 1919, accompanied by the Capuchin Provincial, Padre Pietro of Ischitella. He only remained a few days, and drew up his report on the 26th of the month. During his short stay he examined Padre Pio several times.

To his credit, in his final report Bignami depicts the friar as having an expression on his face that is "full of goodness and sincerity, which inspire affection . . . that in spite of his apparent weakness he supports fatigue very well. He can, for example, hear confessions for even 15-16 continuous hours without eating. He usually eats little . . . He has a vivacious, gentle, and sometimes wandering look . . ." [9]

His five-page report then proceeds to describe in detail the anatomical and histological characteristics of Padre Pio's wounds. [10] He is struck by the symmetry of the "lesions," that is, that the wounds on the palms and soles are in a corresponding place to those on the opposite sides of the same hands and feet. As for the chest wound, he considers that it is simply the result of a superficial abrasion of the epidermis.

He notices that the skin around the wounds is colored with a halo from tincture of iodine, and this arouses his suspicion. In response to Bignami's questions about the iodine, Padre Pio says he uses it as a disinfectant a couple of times a week or more, and it also helps to lessen the bleeding.

In his report, the professor proposes three hypotheses for the origin of the wounds on Padre Pio. As a positivist, Dr. Bignami only considers natural explanations, ignoring any supernatural possibility.

- They are artificially and voluntarily caused.

- They are the manifestation of a morbid (pathological) state [stato morboso].
- They are partially the product of a morbid state and partially artificial.

He rules out the first option, writing that the "impression of sincerity that Padre Pio has made on me" does not allow him to consider the possibility of deliberate simulation as the cause of the wounds. [11]

Regarding the second hypothesis, he deems that the wounds on the feet and hands have in fact a pathological origin, due to neurotically-caused cell deterioration [necrosi neurotiche], but this cannot explain the unexpected symmetry of the wounds.

Therefore he has recourse to the third hypothesis, which he develops further. "We can in fact think that the lesions as described first began as a pathological condition (multiple 'necrosi neurotiche' of the skin), and then perhaps by a process of unconscious suggestion, they came to completion in a symmetrical form, and are now maintained artificially by a chemical means, for example with tincture of iodine." [12]

Thus, he essentially proposes a three stage process – a pathological origin of the wounds, then the influence of autosuggestion to explain their symmetrical location, and finally the use of a chemical to sustain the wounds over time. It important to note that he does not accuse Padre Pio of intentionally *creating* the wounds by chemical means.

Bignami's report then concludes: "This seems to be the most reliable interpretation of the facts that I have observed. In any case one can affirm that there is nothing in the alterations of the skin as described that cannot be the product of a morbid state and of the action of well-known chemical agents." [13]

**The "Cure"**

As a medical professional Bignami believed that Padre Pio's lesions should respond to clinical treatment. In order to conclusively demonstrate that Padre Pio's "sores" had a natural explanation and were maintained by the application of chemicals such as iodine or carbolic acid, Bignami designed a simple procedure, which he believed would lead to a cure of the lesions.

First, any chemicals found in Padre Pio's room should be removed (the only chemical found there was iodine). Next, the doctor proposed that the friar's wounds on his hands, feet and chest were to be bandaged and securely sealed by reliable witnesses, to prevent any tampering. Each day for eight days the bandages would be changed and resealed, and the progress of the treatment was to be noted.

If the wounds were being maintained by the application of chemicals, then protecting them from external substances with bandages should cause their bleeding and size to diminish significantly. Thus, at the end of the procedure the lesions should be well on their way to being healed.

While Bignami was specifically concerned about Padre Pio's use of iodine, Padre Paolino, the Guardian of the friary, thought carbolic acid [acido fenico] had been applied to the wounds in order to stem their bleeding.[14] Carbolic acid was in fact being used in the monastery at that time to sterilize the needles used for injections to prevent the Spanish Flu.[15]

The Father Provincial of the Capuchins, Pietro Ischitella, agreed to the procedure. Under the precept of obedience, he ordered the monastery's Superior, Padre Paolino, and a small group of priests to implement Dr. Bignami's treatment. Padre Pietro made the friars swear that they would scrupulously follow the directives. The Capuchin friars were extremely willing to undertake this task. Now they would be able to see for themselves the stigmata that Padre Pio was always so careful to conceal even from his brothers in religion. Padre Paolino, as the Superior, could have exempted himself, but would not let the opportunity pass. Three others were chosen to be the "reliable witnesses:" Padres Placido, Ludovico, and Basilio.

Padre Paolino later wrote: "The Father Provincial departed, and the next morning, in the presence of the witnesses, I helped to remove the habit and undershirt, together with Padre Pio's socks; along with the other Fathers, I was able to see quite clearly the mark on his chest and those on the feet and hands..." [16]

He continued, "Thus during the space of eight days every morning we removed the bandages of the preceding day after having verified that the seal was intact, and we put new ones on; and in this way we easily observed the stigmata on Padre Pio, who however suffered immensely in the depths of his heart in exposing these wounds, which he always tried to keep hidden from the eyes of others."

## The Result

"Never had the wounds shed so much blood as in those days," wrote one of the witnesses, Padre Placido, in his memoirs. [17] "In the morning, before he ascended the altar to celebrate Mass, we unbound the hands, and in order to prevent blood from staining the vestments and altar cloths, one of us every so often dried the wounds with a cotton wad."

Each morning the seals and bandages were always found intact. On the eighth and last day so much blood issued from Padre Pio's hands during his Mass that the friars had to send for some handkerchiefs so that the Padre could dry them. Paolino wrote: "It seemed to us that it was a very clear sign from God against the arguments of Professor Bignami." [18]

Not only was there no improvement in the condition of the lesions, but they did not even begin to heal! Instead, the bleeding on the last day was worse than before and the blood had taken on a vivid red color. Also, not only the hands, but each of the wounds bled every day, according to a signed deposition of the witnesses. [19]

The existence and sustained bleeding of the stigmata persisted over time, even when any possible application of chemicals was prevented. This proved very clearly that the duration and condition of the wounds did not depend on iodine, carbolic acid, or any other external substance.

Dr. Bignami had departed the friary before the experiment was over, and it is not known what his reaction was. Rev. Bernard Ruffin's well-respected biography of Padre Pio states: "He never again visited Padre Pio, although rumor had it that years later, when he was paralyzed by a stroke, he asked for Padre Pio's prayers." [20] Ruffin also noted: ". . .while the stigmata never healed, all the other wounds sustained by Padre Pio during the course of his life mended normally." [21]

Less than 2 years after Bignami's cure had failed, the Holy Office sent an Apostolic Visitor to San Giovanni Rotondo, Bishop Raffaello Carlo Rossi. He was the Vatican's official Inquisitor into the person, stigmata, phenomena and environment surrounding Padre Pio. His final report and its accompanying documentation comprised almost 200 pages, and had been kept secreted in the Vatican archives until its release in 2006. In it, Bishop

Rossi stated this about the stigmata: "We can then conclude that they were not caused or preserved with physical and chemical means, which, after all, would have been in absolute contrast with Padre Pio's proven virtue . . ." [22]

Not surprisingly, the book which ignited the current carbolic acid controversy (see note 1) devotes only one paragraph to Bignami's attempt at a cure. It does not offer comments on the results and neglects to draw the obvious conclusion. Of course, doing so would have blunted the impact of its sensationalist innuendos, which served to arouse suspicions that Padre Pio had used carbolic acid on his wounds – an allegation which has never been proven.

Padre Pio himself testified about this to the Apostolic Visitor, after taking a solemn oath upon the Holy Gospels to tell the truth. The Bishop pointedly asked him whether he had ever used carbolic acid on himself, either diluted or pure. The saint answered: "No, except when the doctor used it to sterilize when he would give me an injection." [23]

To understand the actual truth about Padre Pio's stigmata, one must rise to the level of faith. While in ecstasy on the morning of September 20, 1918, he witnessed his risen

Savior hovering before him, "dripping with blood and shining forth rays of light and flame" from the wounds of His crucifixion. "When the vision disappeared he found himself on the floor and saw that his own hands, feet and side were dripping blood. He managed to crawl and drag himself back to his cell, unable to walk because of the pain in his pierced feet. He cleansed the wounds, and then remained alone in his room in prayerful weeping and thanksgiving." [24]

No, St. Padre Pio was not a fraud who "faked" his stigmata. Rather, they were a gift from the Lord, given to Padre Pio as a share in His Passion, for his own sanctification, for the salvation of souls and for the glory of God.

### The Players

- Dr. Amico Bignami, tenured Professor of Medical Pathology at the Royal University of Rome.
- Padre Pietro of Ischitella, the Provincial of the Capuchin Province to which belonged the Capuchin Friary of Our Lady of Grace at San Giovanni Rotondo.
- Padre Paolino da Casacalenda, the Guardian (the Superior) of the Friary,

and one of the four witnesses to the "cure."
- Padre Basilio da Mirabello Sannitico, witness.
- Padre Ludovico da San Marco in Lamis, witness.
- Padre Placido da San Marco in Lamis, witness.

## Notes

This article was featured in the June 2012 edition of "Catholic Family News," and in the Fall 2012 issue of "The Voice of Padre Pio,"

1. Luzzatto, Sergio, *Padre Pio: Miracles and Politics in a Secular Age*, New York, Metropolitan Books, 2010.
2. "McGill Prize Honours Book on Padre Pio," www.montrealgazette.com.
3. "Italy's Padre Pio 'faked his stigmata with acid'," www.telegraph.co.uk.
4. "Padre Pio's 'Stigmata Wounds' Caused By Carbolic Acid, Sergio Luzzatto's New Book Suggests," www.huffingtonpost.com.
5. "The Padre Pio Question and Bias in the Media," www.panoramaitalia.com.
6. "Padre Pio and carbolic acid. Could the saint really have been a fraud?" http://blogs.telegraph.co.uk/news/damianthompson/.
7. Di Flumeri, Padre Gerardo, *Le Stigmate di Padre Pio da Pietrelcina*, San Giovanni Rotondo, Edizioni Padre Pio da Pietrelcina, 1995, p. 173.
8. Saldutto, Gerardo, *Un Tormentato Settennio Nella Vita di Padre Pio da Pietrelcina*, San Giovanni Rotondo, Edizioni Padre Pio da

Pietrelcina, 1986, p. 115.
9. Cruchon, Giorgio, "The Stigmata of Padre Pio," in *Acts of the First Congress of Studies on Padre Pio's Spirituality*, San Giovanni Rotondo, Edizioni Padre Pio da Pietrelcina, 1973, p. 124.
10. *Le Stigmate*, pp.. 173-179.
11. *Ibid.*, p. 177.
12. *Ibid.*, p. 178.
13. *Ibid.*, pp. 178-179.
14. *Ibid.*, p. 81.
15. Rega, Frank M., *Padre Pio and America*, Rockford, TAN Books and Publishers, 2005, p. 55.
16. *Le Stigmate*, p. 83.
17. *Ibid.*, p. 72.
18. *Ibid.*, p. 84.
19. *Ibid.*, p. 64.
20. Ruffin, C. Bernard, *Padre Pio: The True Story*, Huntington, Our Sunday Visitor, 1991, p. 177.
21. *Ibid.*, p. 165.
22. Castelli, Francesco, *Padre Pio Under Investigation*, San Francisco, Ignatius Press, 2011, p. 118.
23. *Ibid.*, p. 204.
24. *Padre Pio and America*, Pp. 54-55.

## Chapter Two

## Padre Pio and the General – A Study in Bilocation

It is a little known fact, even among Padre Pio devotees, that not long before he received the visible stigmata in 1918, he was drafted into the Italian army. But the tenure of the great saint's tour of duty during World War I was greatly shortened by his chronic ill-health. He was declared fit only for non-combat duty within Italy, and was assigned to the Medical Corps, where the sickly and very unhappy private was only considered capable of menial tasks such as janitorial duties. He was repeatedly hospitalized and given more than one leave-of-absence for convalescence because of his incurable lung-related infirmities. In fact, the total time of his active duty amounted to only one hundred eighty-two days over a two and one-half year period. [1]

During the summer and fall of 1917, he was assigned to the military barracks at Naples, which at that time was under the overall command of General Luigi Cadorna, Chief of Staff. Cadorna was engaged on the northern front, personally leading hundreds of thousands of Italian troops that had been stalemated for years on the Austrian-Italian frontier. Then, on October 24, 1917, the German forces combined with the Austrians to launch a surprise attack along the front, culminating in the infamous battle of Caporetto. It was a disastrous defeat for the Italians, who had to retreat south almost to Venice. Their staggering loses included forty thousand casualties, with almost three hundred thousand troops taken prisoner, and even more than that number fleeing in retreat.

The Italian lines finally held on November 7 at the Piave River, but on the next day the monarchy relieved Cadorna of his command, replacing him with Armando Diaz as Chief of Staff. The battle of Caporetto is considered the most humiliating military defeat in Italian history. On the 9$^{th}$ of the month, Cadorna packed his bags and prepared to leave for Rome.

The war would not end for another year. There were still major battles to be fought even after Padre Pio, now back in his friary, received the wounds of the stigmata at San Giovanni Rotondo in September of 1918. Then came Armistice Day on November 11 of that year, and a few months later the Paris peace talks began at Versailles. In spite of his clouded reputation, General Cadorna was appointed as one of the members of the Italian military delegation. However, in 1919 in the midst of the peace talks, the official state inquiry into the Caporetto defeat was released, and the blame was laid squarely on Cadorna. He was recalled from the Versailles negotiations, and returned to Italy in disgrace. [2]

It was during the period of time between Cadorna's defeat at Caporetto and his shameful recall from Versailles, that Padre Pio is said to have appeared in bilocation to the General.

Cadorna was alone in his quarters, understandably depressed and in desperate straits because of his public humiliation. With his head bowed in his hands and consumed by his own anguish, he grieved over all of the young men under his command whose lives were lost in the futile campaigns. Suddenly, he was blanketed by a strong aroma of roses that completely penetrated his room. Cadorna raised his head, and was amazed to see before him a friar, whose angelic countenance sharply contrasted with the appearance of his hands, which seemed to be bleeding. Coming closer to the General, the friar tried to reassure him with the words, "Stay calm, and don't do anything drastic." Then, as quickly as he had appeared, the friar was gone, and with his departure the perfume of roses also disappeared.

Not long afterwards, the General confided his experience to a Franciscan priest. As soon as the perfume of flowers was mentioned, the priest said, " Your excellency, you have seen Padre Pio!" The priest then proceeded to explain to him the story of the stigmatized Capuchin friar. The General conceived the desire to see this friar in person, and some months later visited San Giovanni Rotondo. He arrived incognito, dressed in civilian clothing, and had told no one beforehand of his journey. But two Capuchins who recognized him came forward, and announced that Padre Pio was expecting him, and that they had been sent by the friar to greet him.

## The Original Source

Thus concludes the earliest version of this story that the present author has been able to discover. It was written for a Catholic periodical in Italy in January of 1943, probably by Alberto del Fante. It appears in two places in del Fante's classic (untranslated) six-hundred page treatise on the saint, *Per la Storia: Padre Pio di Pietrelcina, Il Primo Sacerdote Stigmatizzato* (For the Sake of History: Padre Pio of Pietrelcina, the First Stigmatized Priest.) [3]

Unlike later accounts of this story by other authors, dating from the 1950's, del Fante provides the reader with the names of some of his sources. He cites Signora Crusiani, the wife of General Venturi, and Signora Zoboli Francesca of Bologna as "persons worthy of belief," and states that the story also comes from "others."

He does not propose an exact date for the occurrence, while later writers are confident that it took place in October or November of 1917, at the time of the Caporetto defeat. Italian writer Renzo Allegri is more specific, citing the evening of November 9, which was the date Cadorna had to pack up and leave for Rome.[4] Even the official biography of St. Pio, written by Fr. Fernando da Riese Pio X and published by the friary in San Giovanni Rotondo, places the event in November. [5] However, as pointed out by C. Bernard Ruffin in *Padre Pio: the True Story*, there are "major problems" with the 1917 dates. Padre Pio is said to have appeared to the General as a friar with bleeding hands, yet he did not receive the visible, bleeding stigmata until a year later, on September 20, 1918.

Some interesting additions creep into the story in the more recent accounts. In most of them, Cadorna is said to have taken a pistol from his night table, and was preparing to shoot himself. [6,7] It was Padre Pio who prevented the suicide. Supposedly, sentries outside the General's quarters had been ordered not to let anyone in to see him, and afterwards the General rushed outside demanding to know from the guards why they had let the friar pass. One version offers even more specific details, saying it was raining that night, that Cadorna opened a window because the perfume was so strong, and that after the incident, he put the pistol back in its holster, closed the window, and went to bed. [8]

## Later Embellishments

Many of the later embellishments appear to stem from the account given by Maria Winowska in her highly acclaimed *The True Face of Padre Pio*, first published in France in 1955. She was a close friend of Mary Pyle's, the American heiress who became Padre Pio's spiritual daughter and built a home next to the friary. Pyle was a gold mine of information on the saint, and Winowska had spent considerable time at her home. Her book is one of the references cited for the Cadorna incident in the friary's official biography. Winowska mentions the suicide attempt, the revolver, the sentries, and that the General was in a tent, but says nothing about the stigmata or bleeding hands. She does not actually give a date for the incident in the English translation of her book. But she does mention that it occurred on November 9, 1917 in the Italian version, [9] and also in a later article she wrote for a Polish magazine. [10]

Winowska writes that on Cadorna's incognito trip to the monastery (she does not mention the two friars who came to greet him), he was informed that it would be impossible to personally see Padre Pio because of "doctors' orders." However, he was told that he could stand in the corridor with others who were waiting for him to pass by. The General hid in a corner, and as the friar passed, he recognized Pio as the protagonist of the nocturnal visit during the war. The Capuchin smiled at him and raised a finger, as if to say "You had a lucky escape, my friend." [11]

Winowska offers no date for the monastery encounter. On the other hand, some important sources, including Fr. Fernando Riese in the official biography, and C. Bernard Ruffin in his American biography, give the year of the visit as 1920. [12,13] Italian author Renzo Allegri also cites the same year. Allegri states that Cadorna had first heard about Padre Pio from newspaper accounts, and recognized him from his picture. Deciding to visit the monastery, he saw a group of friars and identified Padre Pio as the one who had appeared to him. Then, according to Allegri and many other sources, Padre Pio came up to him and said, "We went through a bad time that night!" *("Generale, l'abbiamo passata veramente brutta quella notte!")* [14, 15, 16, 17] Another book gives this version: "Hello General! We escaped by the skin of our teeth that night, didn't we!" [18]

Ruffin notes that overall, the story of Padre Pio's bilocation to General Cadorna is "considered genuine." [19] The presence of the story in the official biography also bestows an imprimatur. However, Ruffin does remark that the story appears to have been embellished, and the original source "is difficult to trace." [20]

The suicide attempt, the revolver, and his anger at the sentries for letting Pio pass, might be no more than literary trappings based on logical assumptions. But why would Padre Pio bother to appear to him unless Cadorna had contemplated taking of his own life? Since he was a soldier, using a gun and the presence of sentries do seem reasonable conclusions.

**Establishing the Date**

The date of the bilocation is never firmly established. Sources that do give a date in October or November of 1917 are probably assuming that his defeat at Caporetto would make that time period the logical choice. However, the mention of the friar's bleeding hands in the early del Fante account runs counter to accepting a 1917 date. Del Fante in fact does not give a year, but says it occurred "during the other war." Further, he says it was only "some months later" that Cadorna went to San Giovanni Rotondo. [21]

If the many accounts which report that he visited the friary in 1920 are true, then it is quite possible that the bilocation occurred in 1919, after Cadorna's public humiliation at Versailles. This disgrace of being specifically blamed for the Caporetto debacle in the official report of inquiry, and his recall from the Paris peace talks, probably marked a lower point in his life than the defeat in battle itself. A 1919 date for that "brutal night" explains both the description of Pio's bleeding hands, and Cadorna's arrival in San Giovanni "some months later," in 1920. A 1917 date would mean an arrival *some years later*, and explaining the bleeding hands becomes a problem.

In view of the above considerations, a bare-bones vignette of the entire incident can be sketched. This scenario draws mainly but not entirely on the del Fante report, which is the oldest and most reliable:

> One evening in 1919, soon after the issue of the official Italian state inquiry blaming him for the Caporetto defeat, General Luigi Cadorna contemplated

suicide in his quarters. Just then, he sensed a strong perfume of roses, followed by the sudden appearance of a friar with bleeding hands and angelic countenance, who deterred him from the deed. Some months later, in 1920, Cadorna traveled incognito to the monastery at San Giovanni Rotondo, after learning that the friar might have been Padre Pio. Though he had told no one about his journey, two Capuchin friars greeted him, claiming they were sent by Padre Pio. As Padre Pio passed before the pilgrims who were waiting to see him, he recognized the General, and spoke a few words to him about that terrible night.

# Notes

This article was featured in the November 2011 edition of "Catholic Family News," and in the January-February 2012 issue of "The Voice of Padre Pio," published by his Friary.

1. Rega, Frank M., *Padre Pio and America,* Rockford, Il., 2005, pp. 40-46.
2. "Cadorna, Luigi" *Encyclopædia Britannica* from Encyclopædia Britannica Premium Service. http://www.britannica.com/eb/article?tocId=9001549.
3. Del Fante, Alberto, *Per la Storia: Padre Pio di Pietrelcina, Il Primo Sacerdote Stigmatizzato,* (hereafter *del Fante*), Bologna, 1949, p. 127; p. 437.
4. Allegri, Renzo, *I Miracoli di Padre Pio* (hereafter *Allegri*), Milan, 1993, p. 109.
5. Fernando da Riese Pio X, *Padre Pio da Pietrelcina: Crocifisso Senza Croce,* (Hereafter *Riese*), San Giovanni Rotondo, 2002, p. 192.
6. Cataneo, Pascal, *Padre Pio Gleanings*

(hereafter *Cataneo*), Quebec, 1991, p. 86.
7. *Allegri*, p. 109.
8. Alimenti, Dante, *Padre Pio*, Bergamo, 1984, p. 83.
9. De Santis, Sergio, "Il Santo e il Macellario," www.cicap.org/ufficiostampa/cs_000908.htm.
10. Lacialamella, Myriam Frisoli, *Voce di Padre Pio*, Vol. XI, no. 9, 1980, p. 30.
*11.* Winowska, Maria, *The True Face of Padre Pio* (hereafter *Winowska*), London, 1961, p. 108.
12. *Riese*, p. 192.
*13.* Ruffin, Bernard, *Padre Pio: The True Story (Revised and Expanded)* (hereafter *Ruffin*), Huntington, IN, 1991, p. 146.
*14. Allegri*, p. 110.
*15. Riese*, p. 192.
*16. Ruffin*, p. 146.
*17. Voice of Padre Pio*, Vol. XIX, no. 3, 1989, pp. 6-7.
*18. Cataneo*, p. 87.
*19. Ruffin.*, p. 325.
*20. Ibid.*, p. 146.
*21. del Fante*, p. 127.

# Chapter Three

## Padre Pio: A Patron Saint for the Unborn

*The Blessed Mother said to him: "I am entrusting this unborn child to your care and protection."*

While two patron saints are generally invoked for the protection of the unborn, St. Joseph and St. Gerard Majella, neither is specifically assigned by the Church for that cause. St. Gerard is in fact the Patron of Expectant Mothers, and by accommodation becomes a patron for the unborn. St. Joseph has often been proposed as a patron saint of the unborn, because of his role as protector of the Holy Family and patron of the Universal Church. However, St. Padre Pio has a specific claim to this honor, a prerogative that was confirmed by the Blessed Virgin Mary herself.

The story begins in 1905, well before he became famous for his stigmata and other spiritual gifts. At that time he was still a seminarian, known as Brother Pio, and was assigned to the humble friary of St. Elia a' Pianisi, in southern Italy. After his involvement in an unusual and striking spiritual encounter, Brother Pio immediately wrote everything down and handed it to his spiritual director, Padre Agostino. The note eventually became part of the documentation presented to the Vatican during the process of his canonization over seventy-five years later. Here is the relevant part of that note (the full note is presented in chapter 10).

Several days ago I had an extraordinary experience. About 11:00 in the evening [of January 18, 1905] Brother Anastasio and I were in the choir. Suddenly I found myself at the same time in the palace of an extremely wealthy family. The master of the house was dying just as his daughter was about to be born.
Then the Blessed Mother appeared and, turning to me, said, "I am entrusting this unborn child to your care and protection. Although she will become a precious jewel,

right now she has no form. Shape and polish her. Make her as brilliant as you can, because one day I would like to adorn myself with her."

Until now, this note has been considered important primarily because it is the first documented instance of St. Pio's supernatural gift of bilocation. However, in the light of today's battle against the abortion holocaust, another aspect of the note takes on added significance. That is, the words of the Blessed Virgin to Brother Pio: "I am entrusting this unborn child to your care and protection."

What greater recommendation could there possibly be for Padre Pio to be the patron saint of the unborn, than that given by the Blessed Mother herself? She specifically entrusted the care of an infant still in her mother's womb, and whose father lay dying, to a young seminarian destined to become one of the greatest saints in the history of the Church. Furthermore, she called this girl about to be born a child; she was not a lump of flesh or a blob of tissue, whose life could be legally snuffed out in today's world by a heinous partial birth abortion procedure.

The name of the child was Giovanna Rizzani. Our Lady had predicted that Padre Pio would meet Giovanna in St. Peter's Basilica, and this came to pass in 1922. It was another case of bilocation, where an "unknown friar" heard her confession and resolved her doubts about the faith. The next year, Giovanna came to San Giovanni Rotondo and she realized that Padre Pio was the friar who had heard her confession in Rome. At this latest encounter, Padre Pio explained to her the vision and supernatural events of 1905 when he witnessed her father's death. He explained that the Virgin Mary had entrusted her to him in order to direct and perfect her soul.

For the next forty-five years, until Padre's passing in 1968, Giovanna visited him often for spiritual direction, and confessed almost exclusively to him. On one occasion she asked him, "Padre, do you really care for me? He replied: "How could I not care for you. You are the first born of my heart. Love Jesus. Love Our Lady, who thought of you before you were born!" [1,2,3]

## Abortion: "That's Killing!"

Padre Pio's horror of abortion is made clear in an incident told to one of his biographers, Rev. Bernard Ruffin, and recounted in the book *Padre Pio: The True Story*. [4] Ruffin had interviewed a gentleman named Albert Cardone, who stated that he had learned of Padre Pio from a woman who had gone to the saint for confession. After the woman had enumerated all the sins she could recall, Padre Pio asked her, "Try to remember the other sin." She said that she could not think of anything more, and Padre Pio told her to visit the cross that is at the top of the mountain, and to recite fifteen Ave Maria's and Our Fathers as a penance. She then returned to Padre Pio's confessional a second time, and he asked her if she remembered all of her sins. She insisted that she remembered all of them, but the Padre replied, "No, you still don't remember all." He sent her once again to the cross on the mountain. The scenario was repeated a third time, and she still did not recall any other sins. Finally, in a loud voice, Padre Pio said, "Don't you know he could have been a good priest, a bishop, even a cardinal?"

The poor woman began to cry, exclaiming that she did not know abortion was a sin. The saint countered with, "What do you mean, you didn't know that this was a sin? That's killing!" The woman said that no one had been told of the abortion except for her mother, and asked how he could say that the child would have been a priest or a cardinal. Padre Pio answered by repeating, "But it's a sin, a great sin." In other words, it did not matter what his position in life would have been.

The Padre Pio literature is replete with stories of infertile couples asking Padre's intercession for the grace of childbirth. The following story is typical.

> During confession, among other things, I manifested to him my great desire to become a father. I had been married for three years, but my wife had not succeeded in having a child. I had her visit the most famous specialists and all of them said that we had to resign ourselves to the situation. There was no other alternative but to ask for a miracle from Padre Pio, and I did so. He replied to me: 'Do not worry about this, for within a year you will become a father.' Although I

realized that to believe in these words meant denying the medical evidence, my heart was filled with joy. As the Padre had predicted, in 1944 I became the father of a lovely little girl. [5]

It is important to note here that Padre Pio never attributed miraculous cures and occurrences to himself, but always to the grace of God and his Virgin Mother. Often he would even successfully predict whether the child would be a boy or a girl.

One day an officer in the Carabinieri (State Police) and his expectant wife visited Padre Pio. He asked the saint what name they should give to the soon-to-be-born baby.

"Name him Pio."
"And what if it is a girl?"
"*I said, call him Pio!*"
When the time arrived, the newborn boy was given the name of Pio.
Two years later, the same officer went to San Giovanni Rotondo to ask Padre Pio what they should name their second child, who was expected shortly.
"Call him Francesco."

"But Padre, I grant that you were right last time, but what if it is a girl?"
*"Man of little faith!"*
A beautiful child was born, and given the name Francesco. [6]

Padre Pio is currently known as the patron saint of civil defense volunteers, after a group of 160 them petitioned the Italian Bishops' conference. The Bishops forwarded the request to the Vatican, which gave its approval to the designation. [7] He is also "less officially" known as the patron Saint of stress relief and the "January blues," after the Catholic Enquiry Office in London proclaimed him as such. They designated the most depressing day of the year, January 22, as *Don't Worry Be Happy* day, in honor of Padre Pio's famous advice: "Pray, hope, and don't worry." [8]

Perhaps the latter patronage is a little tongue-in-cheek, but that of the civil defense volunteers is quite legitimate. It is significant to note that it only took 160 signatures for the Vatican to give its official approval to that designation.

Incidentally, Padre Pio believed 8 children was an ideal family size.

## Notes

This article was featured in the November 2008 edition of "Christian Order."

1. D'Apolito, Padre Alberto, *Padre Pio of Pietrelcina,* San Giovanni Rotondo, Italy, Our Lady of Grace Friary, 1986, pp. 275-296.
2. D,Apolito, Padre Alberto, "Protected by P. Pio all of her life," *The Voice of Padre Pio,*" Volume III, no. 1, 1973, pp. 7-9.
3. Schug, Fr. John A., *A Padre Pio Profile,* Petersham MA., St. Bede's Publications, 1987, pp. 14-30.
4. Ruffin, Rev. C. Bernard, *Padre Pio: The True Story,* Huntington, IN., Our Sunday Visitor, 1991, pp. 296-297.
5. Allegri, Renzo, *Padre Pio, Il santo dei miracoli,* Milano, Mondadori, 2002, p, 311, present writer's translation.
6. Del Fante, Alberto, *Per La Storia,* Bologna, Anonima Arti Grafiche, 1949, p. 474, present writer's translation.
7. "Italy makes St. Padre Pio patron of civil defense volunteers,"

http://www.georgiabulletin.org/world/2004/03/30/WORLD-1/
8. "Saint Pio of Pietrelcina, Popular Veneration" http://www.bbc.co.uk/religion/religions/christianity/saints/pio.shtml

## Chapter Four

## The Pope, Padre Pio, and a Miracle

In the early 1960's Angelo Battisti held two important positions in the Church. He was the administrator for Padre Pio's hospital, the Casa Sollievo Della Sofferenza, located just across the piazza from the Capuchin friary at San Giovanni Rotondo. In addition, he worked in the offices of the Vatican Secretary of State. Shuttling back and forth between Rome and San Giovanni was a weekly occurrence for Battisti, and he was known to be a close personal friend of Padre Pio's. Thus, it was not altogether unusual when in November of 1962 he was asked by a colleague in the secretariat, Guglielmo Zannoni, to deliver an urgent letter to Padre Pio. The letter had been passed on to Zannoni by a Polish monsignor who would eventually become Cardinal Andrej Deskur.[1,2] But this important letter was not written by Deskur himself. Instead, it was composed by another Polish prelate, a bishop from Krakow by the name of Karol Wojtyla.

Bishop Wojtyla was in Rome as a member of the Polish episcopate that was attending the opening session of the Second Vatican Council, which had convened in October. Not long after his arrival in Rome, he received disturbing news about a close friend and collaborator, Dr. Wanda Poltawska. Wojtyla had known Poltawska and her husband Andrei from his earliest days as a priest in Krakow. She had been very active in various Catholic youth movements in Poland prior to the Second World War. But when the Nazis came to power, she was arrested and imprisoned for five years in a concentration camp, where she underwent intense sufferings. Along with other Catholic women, she was forced to submit to "medical experiments" performed by Nazi doctors at the camp. [3]

After the war, she resumed her university studies and her involvement with Catholic youth. At that time, Karol Wojtyla was assigned by his superiors to Saint Florian parish, in the center of Krakow, where he was in charge of the student chaplaincy. This enabled him to personally reach out to the younger men and women. One of ways he did this was by holding conferences to discuss theology and philosophy, areas in which he was already degreed. The popularity of his conferences drew a large following, including the young couple, Wanda and Andrei, who were pursuing careers in medicine and philosophy respectively. [4]

The bond between the new prelate and those who attended his talks and discussions was cemented by his charisma, intelligence, and warmth. He became the spiritual leader and mentor of a close circle of friends. Soon, small groups of students, inspired to learn more about the humanitarian, social, and religious discussions that Wojtyla led, joined him on week-long mountain retreats, which included kayaking and camping. Although Poland was under soviet communist domination, they celebrated Mass together in the open, which was forbidden by the regime. [5] These excursions were held a few times each year.

Dr. Wanda Poltawska was a specialist in family issues, and made important contributions to Wojtyla's early thought on family matters. [6] After he had become Bishop of Krakow, she assisted him in founding an Institute for the Family at the Curia. Many of her ideas were incorporated in his first non-fiction book *Love and Responsibility* in 1960, and eventually influenced Pope Paul VI's encyclical *Humanae Vitae*. [7]

While still a young man, Karol Wojtyla had lost both of his parents and his brother, and had no real family of his own. But his loneliness was assuaged by the deepening of his friendship with the Poltawskas. The couple's own family life had been enriched with children, and eventually Wanda and Andrei were blessed with four young ones. Wojtyla was so close to them that they grew up calling him their "uncle."

As the years progressed, he earned two doctorates, became a university professor, and eventually was nominated Auxiliary Bishop of Krakow. Then, while participating in the Second Vatican Council in Rome, he received the tragic news from his adopted family that Wanda had been diagnosed with an intestinal tumor. The doctors had decided to operate, and if the growth were cancerous, she was given only eighteen months to live. [8] They also told her that there was a ninety-five percent chance that the tumor was malignant.

When the news that his close friend and collaborator had been hospitalized reached Bishop Wojtyla, he immediately began to ask for prayers from his fellow priests, his friends, and religious sisters. Wojtyla prayed intensely that further tragedy would not strike this woman, who had endured five cruel years in a concentration camp. Dr. Poltawska was only forty years old, and her four children still needed her. The Polish bishop's thoughts soon turned to a man he had not seen for fifteen years, a man whose sanctity and prayers he greatly respected.

## Karol Wojtyla's visit to Padre Pio

In the long-ago summer of 1947, Wojtyla had been a priest for less than a year. He was in Rome in the midst of a two-year study program, working on his first doctorate. Extremely interested in Carmelite spirituality and mysticism, he had chosen for his dissertation topic the mystical theology of Saint John of the Cross. It was in Rome that he first heard about another Catholic mystic, a Capuchin rather than a Carmelite, whose fame had not yet spread beyond the iron curtain into Poland. He was said to bear the wounds of Christ, the only priest ever to do so, and he lived only a half-day's journey by train and bus from Rome.

During a break in the school year, Wojtyla decided to visit this modern-day mystic, Padre Pio of Pietrelcina. He spent almost a week in San Giovanni Rotondo that summer, and was able to attend Padre Pio's Mass and make his confession to the saint. Apparently, this was not just a casual encounter, and the two spoke together at length during Wojtyla's stay. [9] Their conversations gave rise to rumors in later years, after the Polish prelate had been elevated to the Papacy, that Padre Pio had predicted he would become Pope. The story persists to the present day, even though on two occasions "Papa Wojtyla" denied it. In 1984, the Capuchin Minister General, Bishop Flavio Carraro personally asked him about the prediction. Also Monsignor Riccardo Ruotolo, president of Pio's hospital, The House for the Relief of Suffering, asked the same question of the Pope three years later. On both occasions the Holy Father emphatically denied that Padre Pio had made such a prophecy. [10]

Back in Rome, the news reaching Bishop Wojtyla about the condition of his dear friend Wanda Poltawska continued to be ominous. A major operation to stem the growth in her intestine now loomed a few days hence. With no time to lose, he took pen in hand and hastily wrote a short, urgent letter to Padre Pio in Latin. The letter, written on the official stationery of the diocese of Krakow, was dated November 17, 1962. Brief and to the point, the Bishop pleaded:

> Venerable Father, I ask for your prayers for a certain mother of four young girls, who lives in Krakow, Poland (during the last war she spent five years in a German concentration camp), and now her health and even her life are in great danger due to cancer. Pray that God, through the intercession of the Most Blessed Virgin, has mercy on her and her family. Most obligated in Christ, Karol Wojtyla. [11]

Since it was essential that the letter arrive as soon as possible, Bishop Wojtyla, acting through intermediaries, enlisted the help of Angelo Battisti in order to have it hand-delivered to Padre Pio. Battisti's positions at the Vatican Secretary of State and as the administrator for Pio's hospital, guaranteed him virtually unlimited access to the saint at almost any hour. He was told that the letter was of utmost importance, and was asked to leave at once and deliver it personally to Pio. The hastily summoned messenger later remarked: "I had never received such an urgent assignment. I quickly went home to get my car, and departed immediately." [12]

## This One Cannot be Refused!

Battisti drove to the friary at San Giovanni Rotondo and headed straight for Padre Pio's room. There he found the priest seated with his head bowed over his chest, engrossed in prayer. The messenger held out the envelope, explaining that it dealt with a pressing matter. Without moving, Pio simply replied, "Open it and read it." He listened in silence as Angelo Battisti read the letter, and remained silent for some time afterwards. Battisti was now surprised that this missive had to be urgently delivered; it seemed to be similar to the torrent of grave requests about life and death matters that daily reached Padre Pio, imploring his prayers. Finally, the Padre raised his head, and with a serious demeanor turned towards the messenger. "Angelo, to this one [questo] it is not possible to say no!" Then he bowed his head as before and resumed praying.

Battisti understood that by using the term "questo", a masculine pronoun, Pio was referring to the person (this one) who sent the letter. On the drive back to Rome, he thought about the many years he had known Padre Pio, and how every single word he wrote or spoke was carefully chosen and had a profound significance. He did not use the feminine "questa," which would have referred to the request or to the letter itself. No, it was "questo" – he who sent it – that could not be refused. But who was this Polish Bishop? Though Battisti worked at the Secretariat of State, he never heard of him. Nor, he found out when he arrived at the Vatican, had any of his colleagues ever heard of Bishop Wojtyla. Yet, why had Padre Pio considered him so important? [13]

The operation to remove the tumor in Dr. Poltawska's intestine was to take place on a Friday in late November 1962. On Saturday, Bishop Wojtyla telephoned the sick woman's husband Andrei to learn whether or not the tumor had been malignant. Andrei started to explain that the operation never took place because the doctors had found that there was nothing they could do. The Bishop immediately began to console his friend, believing that the cancer had been declared inoperable. Andrei interrupted: "Oh no, you do not understand...The doctors are confronted with a mystery. They could not find anything." [14] The growth, which had been previously confirmed as present by the doctors, had now completely disappeared! For Bishop Wojtyla, only one explanation for this cure was possible – the prayers that Padre Pio had raised to heaven.

At the time, the Poltawskas knew nothing about their friend's letter to the holy man of the Gargano, and they did not find out until later. In fact, the couple had never heard of Padre Pio, since Poland was still a closed-off Iron Curtain country, and there was little opportunity for them to learn about events in the free world. Thus, at first Wanda attributed the results to the one-in-twenty possibility that it was an inflammation which had healed on its own, and not a tumor at all. [15]

Upon hearing the good news, Bishop Wojtyla composed a second letter to Padre Pio, this time thanking him for interceding before God for this mother of four children. In the letter dated November 28, again in Latin, he clearly attributes the doctors' failure to find any diseased tissue to divine intervention.

Venerable Father, the woman living in Krakow, Poland, and mother of four children, on the 21st of November, prior to the surgical operation, was suddenly cured. Thanks be to God! And also to you Venerable Father, I offer the greatest possible gratitude in the name of the woman, of her husband, and all of her family. In Christ, Karol Wojtyla, Capitular Bishop of Krakow. [16]

Once again the bishop's letter was consigned to Angelo Battisti, with instructions from Vatican officials to immediately carry it to San Giovanni Rotondo. He departed at once, and upon reaching Our Lady of Grace Friary, the messenger approached Padre Pio in his cell. As before, Pio spoke the simple command: "Open it and read." This time Battisti himself was extremely curious, and upon reading aloud "the truly extraordinary and incredible news" he turned to Padre Pio in order to congratulate him. But the friar was immersed in prayer. "It seemed that he had not even heard my voice as I was reading the letter." [17] The minutes passed by in silence, and finally the Padre asked Angelo to keep these letters of Bishop

Wojtyla, because some day they would become very important.

Returning to Rome, Battisti secured the letters in a safe place, and as the years passed, he almost completely forgot about them. Then, after sixteen years, the evening of October 16, 1978 arrived. Gathered with the crowds in front of Saint Peter's Basilica, he waited anxiously for the announcement of the name of the new pope. When he heard the words "Karol Wojtyla," Battisti was stunned. His first thoughts were of the words of Padre Pio from long ago, "Angelo, to this one it is not possible to say no!" – and then tears came to Battisti's eyes. [18]

## Confirmation of the Miracle

Five years after her sudden 1962 cure, Wanda Poltawska had a rare opportunity to travel from communist controlled Poland to Rome. By then information on Padre Pio had begun to reach her from various sources, and she had also learned of the letters sent to him by Wojtyla, asking for his prayers and subsequently thanking him for her healing. But as a medical doctor herself, she was still inclined to believe that the absence of any tumor at the time of the scheduled surgery was due to a mistaken diagnosis. [19] "It seemed too difficult to comprehend a supernatural intervention." [20]

Hoping to learn more about Padre Pio, attend his Mass, and perhaps meet him in person, she journeyed from Rome to San Giovanni Rotondo in May of 1967. Thanks to a friar she had spoken to the day of her arrival, on the next morning she was led through the sacristy to a seat near the altar for Padre Pio's 5:00 AM Mass. She could thus closely observe the Capuchin as he celebrated "...with incredible intensity and with an expression of suffering on his face." [21] To her, Padre Pio's Mass meant much more than the experience of God's presence during the consecration of the Holy Eucharist. She was able to perceive Christ's Passion itself as it was reflected in the sufferings of Padre Pio as the Mass progressed. The stigmatized friar's own agony, the bloodstains from his wounds, the perspiration running from his forehead, all invoked the sense of Christ's own Calvary. "This sacrifice of the altar was truly the representation of the Passion of Christ." [22]

Afterwards, Wanda gathered with many others in the sacristy, waiting to greet the holy

Padre. He passed by quite close to her, walking slowly on his pierced feet. Looking around at the people, he stopped, and then gazed directly at her. A smile then beamed on his face, as he approached nearer, patted her on the head, and said, "Adesso, va bene?" (Now are you all right?). She was speechless! [23] The other women around Dr. Poltawska wondered who she was, since she had been conspicuously singled out by their beloved Padre. All she could say to them was, "I am from Poland." [24]

The moment Padre Pio's eyes met hers, she understood that he recognized her, and now knew for certain why she had not needed an operation several years earlier. It was not because of a wrong diagnosis, but because, "...this monk had come into my life in such an extraordinary way because the Archbishop of Krakow had asked for it." [25] And Padre Pio had known at the time he received the urgent request from Karol Wojtyla that "this one" could not be refused. [26]

## Notes

This article was featured (without footnotes) in two parts, in the December 2007 and January 2008 editions of "Catholic Digest."

1. http://www.catholic.net/RCC/Periodicals/Inside/08-96/padrepio.html. "Padre Pio, Will John Paul II Declare Him A Saint?" archived at www.archive.org.
2. http://www.parrocchie.it/calenzano/santamariadellegrazie/PADREPIO%20PASSATOEPRESENTE.htm. "Con il frate di Pietrelcina il Papa ritrova le energie," by Andrea Tornieli.
3. "Critical Biography for Wanda Poltawska" http://womenineuropeanhistory.org/index.php?title=Critical_Biography_for_Wanda_Poltawska.
4. Allegri, Renzo, *I Miracoli di Padre Pio* (hereafter *Miracoli*), Milan, Oscar Mondadori, 1993, p. 189.
5. "John Paul II" *Encyclopædia Britannica* from Encyclopædia Britannica Premium Service. <http://www.britannica.com/eb/article?tocId=214816>

[Accessed December 14, 2004].
6. *Miracoli*, p. 190.
7. http://www.catholicireland.net/pages/index.php?nd=109&art=128. "The Making of a Pope – III."
8. Ruffin, Bernard, *Padre Pio: The True Story (Revised and Expanded)* (hereafter *Ruffin*), Huntington, IN, Our Sunday Visitor, 1991, p. 360.
9. http://www.medjugorje.it/docs/2002/104/Una%20grande%20amicizia.htm, "Karol Wojtyla e Padre Pio: Una Grande Amicizia," by Renzo Allegri.
10. http://www.calabriaweb.it/Ecclesia/1021465600466.html, "Giovanni Paolo II, devoto del Frate di Pietrelcina," by Raffaele Iaria.
11. *Miracoli*, p. 191, (present author's translation).
12. *Ibid.*, p. 193, (present author's translation).
13. *Ibid.*
14. *Ruffin*, p. 361.
15. Poltawska, Wanda, "Padre Pio the Saint of Our Time," (hereafter *Poltawska*), Lay Witness (Catholics United for the Faith), October 1999, www.cuf.org/oct99b.htm.

16. *Miracoli*, pp. 193-194, (present author's translation).
17. *Ibid.*, p. 195.
18. *Ibid.*
19. www.fides.org/eng/interviste/wanda.html (hereafter *Fides*), Fides Service interview with Dr. Wanda Poltawska, June 6, 2002.
20. *Poltawska.*
21. *Ibid.*
22. *Ibid.*
23. *Ibid.*
24. *Fides.*
25. *Poltawska.*
26. In the Fides Service interview (note 19), Dr. Poltawska is cited as saying that Padre Pio "said nothing" when he encountered her at the Friary in San Giovanni Rotondo. In order to resolve the important discrepancy between the Fides interview and the Lay Witness article (note 15), the present author, thanks to Leon Suprenant and Madeleine Stebbins of Catholics United for the Faith, was able to contact Dr. Poltawska's daughter Ania Dadak. She recalled that as a child she had first heard the story from her mother, who related that Pio had said "Va bene." At the

author's request, Dr. Dadak contacted her mother in Poland, who confirmed that Pio had in fact spoken to her, saying "Adesso, va bene?" She never told the Fides reporter that Padre Pio had kept silent, so evidently she was misquoted.

# Chapter Five

# Padre Pio's Secret: His Shoulder Wound

Shortly after World War II was over, a young Polish priest who was studying in Rome, Fr. Karol Wojtyla, visited Padre Pio in San Giovanni Rotondo. This encounter took place around 1947 or 1948. At that time in post-war Italy, it was possible to have access to Padre Pio, since travel was difficult and great crowds were not besieging the Friary. The young priest spent almost a week in San Giovanni Rotondo during his visit, and was able to attend Padre Pio's Mass and make his confession to the saint. Apparently, this was not just a casual encounter, and the two spoke together at length during Fr. Wojtyla's stay. Their conversations gave rise to rumors in later years, after the Polish prelate had been elevated to the Papacy, that Padre Pio had told him he would become Pope. The story persists to the present day, even though on two or three occasions "Papa Wojtyla" denied it.

However, it has recently come to light, in the new book *Il Papa e Il Frate*, by Stefano Campanella[1], that the future Pope and future Saint had a very interesting conversation. During this exchange, Fr. Wojtyla asked Padre Pio which of his wounds caused the greatest suffering. From this kind of personal question, we can see that they must have already talked together for some time and had become at ease with each other. The priest expected Padre Pio to say it was his chest wound, but instead the Padre replied, "It is my shoulder wound, which no one knows about and has never been cured or treated." This is extremely significant, not only because it reveals that Padre Pio bore this wound, but because, as far as is known, the future pope is the *only one* to whom Padre Pio ever revealed existence of this secret wound.

Centuries earlier, Our Lord himself had revealed to St. Bernard of Clairvaux in a vision, that His shoulder wound from carrying the heavy wooden cross caused him His greatest suffering, and that the cross tore into His flesh right up to the shoulder bone.

At one time, Padre had confided to his *paisano* from Pietrelcina, Brother Modestino Fucci, that his greatest pains occurred when he changed his undershirt. (Brother Modestino was the doorkeeper at Padre Pio's friary in San Giovanni Rotondo, Italy.) Modestino, like Fr. Woltyla, thought Padre Pio was referring to pains from the chest wound. Then, on February 4, 1971 Modestino was assigned the task of taking an inventory of all the items in the deceased Padre's cell in the friary, and also his belongings in the archives. That day he discovered that one of Padre Pio's undershirts bore a circle of bloodstains in the area of the right shoulder. This reminded Brother Modestino that he had once read about a devotion to the shoulder wound of Jesus, caused by His bearing of the heavy cross beam, the *patibulum*, to Calvary. The beam could weigh up to 100 pounds. Part of this devotion to the shoulder wound of Christ is to pray daily three Our Father's, Hail Mary's and Glory Be's, to honor the severe pains and lacerations He suffered from the weight of the *patibulum*.

On that very evening of February 4, 1971, Brother Modestino asked Padre Pio in prayer to enlighten him about the meaning of the bloodstained undershirt. He asked Padre to give him a sign if he truly bore Christ's shoulder wound. Then he went to sleep, awakening at 1:00 AM with a terrible, excruciating pain in his shoulder, as if he had been sliced with a knife up to the shoulder bone. He felt that he would die from the pain if it continued, but it lasted only a short time. Then the room became filled with the aroma of a heavenly perfume of flowers – the sign of Padre Pio's spiritual presence – and he heard a voice saying "Cosi ho sofferto io!" – "This is what I had to suffer!" Modestino remarked that he had a strange sensation after the pain subsided: that being deprived of this pain was also a suffering. His body had suffered from it, but his soul had desired it. He said, "It was painful and sweet at the same time."

What is the mystical and spiritual significance of the shoulder wound of St. Padre Pio? The book by journalist Saverio Gaeta, *Sulla Soglia del Paradiso*[2], reports that Padre Pio said this of his spiritual children: "When the Lord entrusts a soul to me, I place it on my shoulder and never let it go." From this statement, it can reasonably be inferred that the saint offered up the suffering and the extreme pain of his shoulder wound for his spiritual children.

Cleonice Morcaldi once said in the presence of Gaeta, "On the shoulders of Padre Pio rests the whole world and the Church." This expression seemed an exaggeration to the writer. But on the very same day that Gaeta had heard this, he later joined Padre Pio and some others. Padre Pio was telling the story of St. Christopher, and how he had carried the child Jesus on his shoulders across a river. Then, turning his gaze to look directly at Saverio Gaeta, Padre Pio pointedly said to the writer, "On my shoulders is the whole world."

## Notes

This article was featured in the March-April 2008 edition of "The Voice of Padre Pio."

1. Campanella, Stefano, *Il Papa e Il Frate*, San Giovanni Rotondo, Italy, Edizioni Padre Pio da Pietrelcina, 2005.
2. Gaeta, Saverio, *Sulla Soglia del Paradiso*, Edizione speciale per *Famiglia Christiana*, San Paolo Edizioni, 2002.

# Chapter Six

# Padre Pio on Salvation Outside the (Visible) Church

Introductory Note: "Salvation Outside the (Visible) Church," has been revised from the original printed version, and the word "Visible" has been added to the title. This addition is to clarify that all salvation is from the Roman Catholic Church, which is the Body of Christ, but the examples in this article show that Padre Pio felt that not being a formal, visible member of the Church during one's lifetime does not preclude a properly disposed person from being incorporated into the Body of Christ, at the time of death.

It is quite common that alleged quotations or viewpoints attributed to Padre Pio have frequently been used to justify the stances, rumors, or agendas of various individuals or groups. Often it is difficult to find reliable documentation to verify his involvement in such scenarios as the "three days of darkness,"[1] his alleged opposition to Archbishop Marcel Lefebvre, [2] or his purported support of Garabandal [3] and even Medjugorje [4]. Another area of speculation focuses on what he would think of the current state of the Church – where would this Tridentine rite Catholic, known for his lifelong obedience and loyalty to the hierarchy, place his support along the Novus Ordo – Traditionalist – reactionary spectrum?

It is not surprising, then, to find some who contend that St. Padre Pio would be an exacting Traditionalist. Thus he would be expected to hold to a strict interpretation of *extra ecclesiam nulla salus* – outside of the Roman Catholic Church no one can be saved. Among the most notable proponents of this presumed stance of Padre Pio are to be found some Sedevacantists (the See of Peter is vacant, since it has been occupied by invalidly elected and/or heretical popes since Vatican II), as well as the so-called Feeneyites.[5] Along with adherence to the true Faith, and being in a state of grace at the moment of death, they would insist that a strict requirement for entering the kingdom of heaven is water baptism, and water baptism alone. "Baptism of Desire" and "Baptism of Blood" are rejected as not being true Catholic dogmas. Neither can those invincibly ignorant of the Faith be saved.

Thus, according to them, only Roman Catholics who die faithful to the Church, loyal to the Holy Father, and sealed by validly administered water baptism, can enter heaven.

There is a wonderful meditation composed by Padre Pio in which he states: "He [Jesus] sees the sacrileges with which priests and faithful defile themselves, not caring about those sacraments instituted for our salvation as necessary means for it; now, instead, made an occasion of sin and damnation of souls." [6]

From this it can be seen that Padre Pio viewed the sacraments as the "necessary means" of salvation. However, in studying the course of his life and ministry as a Catholic priest, evidence can be found that he understood the sacraments as necessary for all in general, but not for all in particular. Thus, while he believed that the sacraments of the Church are necessary as the normative means of salvation, Padre Pio was willing to admit of exceptions on an individual basis. But these exceptions did not compromise his conviction that the one true Church founded by Jesus Christ is the Roman Catholic Church.

Lest anyone be deceived into joining the Sedevacantist camp under the assumption that Padre Pio would support their views if he were alive today, the following documented cases are presented as evidence that Padre Pio believed that non-Catholics could be saved.

### Adelaide McAlpin Pyle, a Baptized Protestant

*"She will be saved because she has faith."*

Most of the information for this first account comes from the English version of the book *Mary Pyle*, by Bonaventura Massa.[7] This work was diligently compiled from written documents and taped oral testimonies, kept on file in the archives of Padre Pio's friary in anticipation of the process for Miss Pyle's Cause for Beatification.

The wealthy Presbyterian, Adelaide McAlpin Pyle, was the mother of Mary Pyle, a well-known convert to Catholicism who renounced her family fortune in order to spend her life near Padre Pio. The Pyle family was related by marriage to the Rockefellers, and made their fortune in the soap and hotel business. After Adelaide found out that her daughter Mary had chosen to move to southern Italy to learn about God from a saint, curiosity impelled her to travel from her plush New York townhouse to medieval San Giovanni Rotondo, in order to meet this holy man.

In spite of an unpleasant initial encounter, Adelaide eventually became quite friendly with Padre Pio. She made numerous journeys from America, beginning in the mid-1920s, to visit her daughter Mary, and to meet with the Padre. Mary often tried to convince her mother to convert to Catholicism as she herself had done, but Adelaide reportedly said in Padre Pio's presence, "I would rather allow myself to be burned alive for my religion!" Padre Pio advised Mary not to push her mother to convert: "Let her be! Don't upset her peace." [8] However, Mary continued to worry because her mother was not a Catholic, and Padre Pio counseled, "Let's not confuse her. She will be saved because she has faith."[9]

In 1936, Adelaide, who had grown older and was nearing death, made one last trip to San Giovanni Rotondo. As she said good-bye to

Padre Pio at the end of this visit, the saintly priest pointed heavenward, saying to the Protestant Adelaide, "I hope we will see each other again soon, but if we don't see each other here, we will see each other up there."[10] She passed away in the fall of 1937 at the age of seventy-seven.[11] Her daughter Mary then became pre-occupied about her mother's salvation. After dreaming that her mother was in Rome standing in front of the Vatican, she poured out her anxiety to Padre Pio. He replied, "And who told you that your mother could not be saved?" [12]

Did Padre Pio receive a revelation that Adelaide Pyle had secretly *'in pectore"* converted to the Catholic Faith? If that were true, he most certainly would have told this to her daughter Mary, who was obviously distraught from worrying over her mother's salvation. Further, it seems likely that if Adelaide had converted, she would have shared this good news with her convert daughter. It is reasonable to conclude then that Padre Pio believed that this particular person who died outside the Church could be saved. In addition, there is evidence that Padre Pio would have been willing to hear Adelaide's confession, and grant her sacramental absolution. On one occasion, she had confided to her daughter her great desire to kneel before Padre Pio in his confessional, but she lamented that her inability to speak Italian made this impossible. When Padre Pio heard of this, (apparently it was after her death), he bemoaned, "Oh! If she had only done it! As for the language, I would have taken care of that!"[13]

## King George V of England, a Baptized Protestant

*"Let us pray for a soul . . ."*

One evening in 1936 Padre Pio was conversing with some dear friends in his cell. Among those present were Dr. Guglielmo Sanguinetti and Angelo Lupi, who would respectively become the medical director and the builder of Padre Pio's hospital years later. In the middle of their conversation, Padre Pio suddenly interrupted the discourse with the words, "Let us pray for a soul soon to appear before the tribunal of God." With that he bowed his head, and his guests, although astonished, knelt and joined him in prayer. When they had finished, Padre Pio announced that they had been praying for the king of England. The next morning, the news blared forth on the friary radio of the unexpected death of King George V of England the previous evening.[14] Two of the sources for this story [15, 16] report that Padre Aurelio was also present in the room, while another source states that Padre Pio went to the friary cell of Padre Aurelio at midnight that evening and asked him to join him in prayers for the king of England who "at that moment" was to appear before God.[17]

An Anglican and the son of the future King Edward VII, George was baptized on July 7, 1865 in the private chapel of Windsor Castle. Upon accession to the throne in 1910, the new king swore the following required oath: "I, N., do solemnly and sincerely in the presence of God, profess, testify and declare that I am a faithful Protestant, and that I will, according to the true intent of the enactments to secure the Protestant Succession to the Throne of my realm, uphold and maintain such enactments to the best of my power."[18]

In all likelihood, the king was in his final agony or had already died when Padre Pio requested prayers for him, since he was "at that moment" to appear before God. If he believed that the soul of this Protestant were doomed to the everlasting fire, why would he pray for him, and also ask others including another priest to do likewise, other than to ask for his conversion? However, it is not recorded or implied that he asked his confreres to pray for the deathbed conversion of the king – an important intention that Padre Pio in all likelihood would have explicitly stated, if such were his purpose. Although he mentioned the king to his priest colleague, he did not tell the friends in his room that they were praying for a non-Catholic until they had finished their prayers. One cannot therefore say that it is to be assumed that as Catholics they were praying for the king's conversion.

Since as far as is known they were not specifically asked to pray for his deathbed conversion, there are two alternatives. The first is that they were simply praying for the salvation of a Protestant whom Padre Pio did not consider doomed because of his non-Catholic religion. Of course this scenario would not be acceptable to one who holds that Padre Pio subscribed to a literal *extra ecclesiam nulla salus* position. Those who hold that position are left with the unlikely alternative that they were praying for a Catholic, and that Padre Pio had requested the prayers because he was given a private revelation that King George

V of England was secretly a Roman Catholic, loyal to the Pope!

## Julius Fine, an Unbaptized Devout Jew

*"Julius Fine is saved..."*

Fr. Alessio Parente, O.F.M. Cap., lived and worked alongside Padre Pio for many years in Our Lady of Grace Friary at San Giovanni Rotondo. He wrote numerous books about his confrere, and his works provide reliable source material for the saint. The following information is from Fr. Alessio's book *The Holy Souls*, [19] and was related by a "very good friend" of his, Mrs. Florence Fine Ehrman, the daughter of the person in question.

In 1965 her father, Julius Fine, who had practiced the Jewish faith all his life and believed firmly in God, was stricken with what is commonly called "Lou Gehrig's disease." Mrs. Ehrman wrote to Padre Pio beseeching a cure for her father from this fatal illness. A short time later she received the reply that Padre Pio would pray for her father and would take him under his protection.

When her father passed away in February of the next year, she was able to accept his death peacefully. However after some time, she began to worry about whether or not he was saved, even though he had been a very loving and kind husband and father. "This fear came about because I began to hear many people, Protestants and Catholics alike, say that unless person had been baptized they could not be saved."

On a visit to the friary at San Giovanni Rotondo in the fall of 1967, she was told by a personal friend (quite possibly Fr. Alessio himself) to write down whatever she wished to ask Padre Pio, and this friend would present the letter to him. She of course wrote down her concerns about the eternal state of her father's soul – this good and gentle Jewish man who had never been baptized. The reply from Padre Pio, which she received in writing, was this: "Julius Fine is saved, but it is necessary to pray much for him." Her mind was put at ease by such a "sure and definite" statement," since she understood that her father was in Purgatory, his salvation guaranteed.

Whether Padre Pio was enlightened by his Guardian Angel, the Holy Spirit, interior locution, or some other means is not known. What is known, however, is his ability to make such determinations after intense prayer, nourished by his mystical union with Christ during his Mass and Holy Communion, and by the offering up of his sufferings, especially the painful bloody wounds of his stigmata. In this instance, Padre Pio committed himself to assuring a grieving daughter that her father, who was not baptized, and was not a Roman Catholic, was saved. As in the case of King George V, someone who wishes to force Padre Pio into the strict "absolutely no salvation outside the Church" camp, is only left with this improbable scenario: it was revealed to Padre Pio that the devout Jew, Julius Fine, was secretly a baptized Roman Catholic!

## Padre Pio a True Catholic

From the above examples it appears that Padre Pio did not blindly adhere to the proposition that only Catholics can be saved. Yet, it would be difficult to find someone more committed to the Catholic Church throughout his life than was Padre Pio. His obedience to the hierarchy was legendary, and he humbly submitted to Vatican-authorized suppression and even persecution without resistance. The spirituality of his epistles astonished even Carmelites, and his writings and teachings, born of the school of suffering, are the basis of an effort to make him a Doctor of the Church. [20]

Padre Pio lived by the Spirit of God, not by the letter of the law, except when his superiors in religion routinely commanded obedience of him. His ingenuous openness to the plenitude of God's mercy anticipated the explicit declarations of the Church during and after the Second Vatican Council on the possibility that non-Catholic churches can be a "means of salvation,"[21] and on the reception by non-Catholics of the sacraments in certain cases.[22] Padre Pio actually believed that the gospel of Jesus Christ was Good News!

## Notes

This article is a revised and updated version of the one featured in the December 2006 edition of "Christian Order."

1. http://www.spiritdaily.org/New-world-order/threedays.htm. "Recent Outages Bring To Mind Prophecy: Will There Be 'Three Days Of Darkness'?"

2. http://www.sspx.org/archbishop_lefebvre/padre_pio_and_archbishop.htm. "Padre Pio and Archbishop Lefebvre."

3. http://www.garabandal.us/padre_pio.html "Padre Pio Connection."

4. http://ingodscompany2.blogspot.ca/2012/06/padre-pios-prophecies-on-medjugorje_29.html. "Padre Pio's Prophecies on Medjugorje."

5. http://www.sspx.org/miscellaneous/feeneyism/three_errors_of_feeneyites.htm. "The three errors of the Feeneyites."

6. Radio Replies Press, Inc. *The Agony of Jesus*, TAN Books, Rockford, IL. p. 24.

7. Massa, Bonaventura, *Mary Pyle, She Lived Doing Good to All,* San Giovanni Rotondo, Our Lady of Grace Capuchin Friary, 1986.

8. *Ibid.*, p. 101.

9. *Ibid.*, p. 116.

10. *Ibid.*, p. 108.

11. Ruffin, C. Bernard, *Padre Pio: the True Story (Revised and Expanded),* Huntington, IN, Our Sunday Visitor, 1991, p. 240.

12. Massa, *Mary Pyle*, p. 108.

13. *Ibid.*, p. 101.

14. Parente, Fr. Alessio, *The Holy Souls: "Viva Padre Pio,"* San Giovanni Rotondo, Our Lady of Grace Capuchin Friary, 1990, pp. 151-152.

15. Capobianco, Padre Costantino, *Detti e Anedotti di Padre Pio*, San Giovanni

Rotondo, Convento S. Maria delle Grazie, 1996, p. 49.

16. Parente, *The Holy Souls*, p. 151.

17. Ruffin, *Padre Pio*, p. 241, (Ruffin correctly identifies the King who died in 1936 as George V, while the other two sources incorrectly call him Edward VI).

18. http://www.newadvent.org/cathen/13213a.htm. "The Royal Declaration."

19. Parente, *The Holy Souls*, pp. 104-106.

20. Rega, Frank M., *Padre Pio and America*, Rockford, IL, TAN Books and Publishers, Inc., 2005, pp. 280-281.

21. Decree on Ecumenism, *Unitatis Redintegratio*, n. 3, (www.vatican.va) "It follows that the separated Churches and Communities as such, though we believe them to be deficient in some respects, have been by no means deprived of significance and importance in the mystery of salvation. For the Spirit of Christ has not refrained from using

them as means of salvation which derive their efficacy from the very fullness of grace and truth entrusted to the Church."

22. On commitment to Ecumenism, *Ut Unum Sint*, n. 46, (www.vatican.va). "In this context, it is a source of joy to note that Catholic ministers are able, in certain particular cases, to administer the Sacraments of the Eucharist, Penance and Anointing of the Sick to Christians who are not in full communion with the Catholic Church but who greatly desire to receive these sacraments, freely request them and manifest the faith which the Catholic Church professes with regard to these sacraments."

# Chapter Seven

## The Gemma Di Giorgi Mystery

One of the most famous of all of the miraculous healings attributed to St. Pio of Pietrelcina is recounted in the intriguing story of Gemma Di Giorgi. Although she was born blind and without pupils, she attributes the fact that she can see today – still without pupils – to the prayerful intercession of the saint of the Gargano, Padre Pio. The cure aroused considerable interest in the Italian press when it occurred in 1947, appearing in local and national papers. In Milan, the Corriere d'Informazione reported the phenomenon on June 18 and 19, "...with a typically frenzied journalistic heading." [1]

Gemma was born in 1939 on Christmas day in Ribera, a city in the province of Agrigento, Sicily. Her mother soon realized there was something drastically amiss with little Gemma's vision. Suspecting that her child might be blind because her eyes did not seem to have any pupils, she took her three-month old baby to the family doctor. Unable to diagnose her condition, he recommended that Gemma be taken to eye specialists in Palermo. In short order, a number of eye doctors examined her, including three whose names are known: Dr. Cucco, Dr. Contino, and Dr. Bonifacio. Their conclusion was unanimous – the child could not possibly see because she in fact had no pupils. (A pupil is not an eye structure in and of itself. It is actually a 'hole' or opening in the middle of the iris, through which light passes into the interior of the eye. The pupil appears as a black dot of varying size depending on light intensity and age.)

Her anguished parents frequently took Gemma to the altar of the Virgin Mary at their local church in order to pray for a miracle, since the doctors had given no hope of a cure. According to the Di Giorgi's parish priest, Father Gambino, the child was also entrusted to the prayers of her namesake, St. Gemma

Galgani. Gambino speculated that her cure may have initially begun with this entrustment, since at the age of one year, Gemma was apparently "...able to see her parents in a shadowy way when they came close to her." However, for all practical purposes she was still blind. Her eyes looked like large dark circles, "...incapable of movement, this immobility being painfully emphasized by frequent spasmodic convulsions of the eyelids." [2]

Gemma's mother had a cousin, a nun, who visited their home in Ribera when the child was about 8 years old. This nun was devoted to Padre Pio and told the family about the holy monk living in San Giovanni Rotondo, who bore the wounds of Christ. She encouraged them to pray to him, and ask for his help in restoring Gemma's vision. The nun's plea greatly affected Gemma's grandmother, who asked the nun to write to Padre Pio on the child's behalf. Spurred on by this new hope, the grandmother began earnestly praying to the saint for a cure. Apparently the rest of Gemma's family, friends, and relatives also began bombarding Padre Pio with their prayers. For her part, the nun, upon returning to her convent, did write a letter to the Padre asking for his intercession. Later she had a vivid dream, in which she envisioned Padre Pio asking her, "Where is this Gemma for whom so many prayers are being offered that they are almost deafening?" [3] In her dream, the nun introduced the friar to little Gemma. Padre Pio made the sign of the cross over the girl's eyes, and then he vanished.

On the day following the dream, a letter from Padre Pio reached the sister at her convent. In it, the saint had written: "Dear daughter, I assure you of my prayers for the little one. Best Wishes!" [4] Inspired by the remarkable coincidence of the arrival of the letter from the Padre immediately after having the dream about him, the nun wrote at once to the Di Giorgi family, describing the dream and Pio's letter. She exhorted them to visit the saint at his monastery. Upon receipt of this news, preparations were made to have Gemma and her grandmother travel from Sicily to San Giovanni Rotondo. Some time afterwards, the pair left on their journey, accompanied by a group of friends from the area. (Reports of the time that elapsed before the start of the trip vary from the same day the nun's letter arrived to one year later.)

The journey across the southern Italian peninsula was not an easy one, since the destruction left behind by World War II still created obstacles for travelers in the post-war years. At one point, the small group of tired pilgrims was on a train near the seacoast, halfway to their goal. Suddenly, Gemma's vision apparently started to function to some degree. She thought she saw the sea with something on it that looked like the toy boat that her grandmother had her touch at one time. She woke up her sleeping grandmother, exclaiming that she could see something in the water, a "steamship." While some of Gemma's fellow travelers cried out about a miracle and began praying, the grandmother did not believe her. She checked the child's eyes and saw that she still had no pupils, and concluded that the child could not possibly see anything. Gemma reported (in an Italian documentary film made years later), "From that moment I saw clearly..." [5] But in an interview with noted author Renzo Allegri, she stated that she only saw "shadows" on the train trip to San Giovanni. [6]

Their arrival at San Giovanni Rotondo occurred on a late spring morning in 1947. They entered the tiny medieval church of Our Lady of Grace, waiting for Padre Pio to come into the chapel to hear the confessions of the women and girls. The little party had probably arrived too late to attend the saint's 5:00 AM Mass. When Padre Pio made his appearance before the assembled devotees, he reportedly was able to identify Gemma in the crowd, and called her by name, although she had never before been presented to him. [7, 8]

The child made her confession to the stigmatized friar, but completely forgot to ask for the grace of having her vision restored. Although she had not mentioned her problem to the Padre, as she was kneeling before him, he passed his hand over her eyes, making the sign of the cross over each eye. At the end of the confession he told her, "Sii buona e santa." (Be good and saintly.) [9]

Her grandmother had specifically reminded the child to ask Pio to pray for the healing of her eyes during her confession to him, and was quite upset when Gemma told her she had forgotten to do so. Apparently she still did not believe that her granddaughter had been able to see anything from the train window on the ride to the monastery. She approached Padre Pio when the confessions were over (or possibly while confessing to him herself) and explained that Gemma was crying because she had forgotten to ask him for the grace. Pio in gentle and kindly fashion replied: "Do you have faith my daughter? The child must not weep and neither must you for the child sees, and you know she sees." [10] At that moment, the grandmother realized he was referring to Gemma's experience while on the train.

It was the custom for Padre Pio to distribute Communion at mid-day for those who could not attend the early morning Mass. Gemma had not yet made her First Holy Communion, but her grandmother had been preparing her for it. The fortunate Gemma was thus able to receive the sacrament for the first time from the stigmatized hands of the friar. In Gemma's words, "When it was time for Communion, a man took me in his arms and carried me to Padre Pio." [11] After giving her the host, Pio once again traced the sign of the cross over each of her eyes. The date was June 18, 1947.

Gemma recalls that on the return trip to Sicily after visiting Padre Pio, "I had the impression that little by little I was beginning to see." [12] The entire journey was so exhausting for her grandmother that when they reached Cosenza, she was admitted to the municipal hospital with a high fever. They were there for several days, during which she had Gemma examined by the hospital's eye specialist. He immediately pronounced that Gemma would not be able to see because she lacked pupils.

The grandmother became confused and worried – she felt sure that Gemma could see and thought that the child's eyes should therefore now have pupils. The grandmother insisted that tests be performed, which proved to the oculist that Gemma could indeed see. According to the grandmother, the perplexed doctor then stamped his foot on the floor, saying "Without pupils one cannot see. The child sees; therefore it is a miracle." [13] Gemma remembers that he also remarked, "There is no explanation for this. ...I don't understand why this child sees." [14]

Only four months after returning to their hometown of Ribera in Sicily, Gemma was examined by a Dr. Caramazza from Perugia. He too declared that her eyes "...were in no condition to see." [15] Her grandmother reports that since the cure many eye specialists from Italy have requested to examine Gemma's eyes, some of them arriving at her home. All declare the same thing – without pupils she should not be able to see, and therefore it is a "miracle."

Because of her restored vision, Gemma was able to attend school and learned to read and write. "Today my life is as perfectly normal as any other person's life." [16]  She submits to occasional eye exams by specialists, who are amazed that she can see without pupils. She enjoys announcing to them that the prayers and intercessions of Padre Pio obtained the miracle of her sight. As for Padre Pio's part, he has been known to say, "Don't bring me into this, my good people. It was not I, it was the Madonna." [17]

In 1967, author Clarice Bruno (*Roads to Padre Pio*) asked Gemma if she would be willing to be interviewed for her book. Before consenting, Gemma, now a young woman, spoke to Padre Pio in confession and obtained his permission to proceed with the interview. She usually wears dark sunglasses, and had them on during the confession. Pio said to her, as he passed his hands over her eyes, "Why are you wearing glasses? You see very well." [18] Bruno wrote that the eyes of the gracious and attractive girl were "...those foggy, strange looking eyes that are a characteristic of the blind." [19]

To Italian author Renzo Allegri, who interviewed her when she was in her 30's, Gemma remarked, "If you look at me closely, you will notice that my eyes are a little strange." [20] Noted Pio author Fr. John Schug's impression was that "She looks like a blind person. Her eyes are sallow and lusterless. But there is no doubt that she can see." [21] Maria Calandra, whose mother is Vera Calandra, the founder of the National Centre for Padre Pio in Barto, Pennsylvania, has met Gemma often. Maria observes that "She does not have pupils and her eyes are those of a blind person, yet she sees everything. She does wear sunglasses, but inside she did not, that is how I know what her eyes look like. She is a nice person and does not draw attention to herself." [22]

An Italian organization called Cicap (www.cicap.org), which investigates paranormal occurrences with an "eye" towards debunking them, has posted an article on their website by Andrea Salsi.[23] Salsi questions Gemma's insistence on wearing sunglasses when telling her story on television or in public appearances. He implies that if she is completely cured, she should not be hiding her eyes. Apparently, Salsi is thinking like Gemma's grandmother once did – that if she can now see, she must therefore have normal eyes and pupils. He reports, as if uncovering an indication of fraud, that when she does take her glasses off, her eyes "roll" as if they were terribly disturbed by the light. However, since we have seen that her eyes continue to have a strange appearance, it is perfectly normal behavior on her part to cover them with dark glasses.

Cicap, which prides itself on its skepticism, asks via Salsi's article if this cure is truly a prodigy. Perhaps, they speculate, it is a case of "spontaneous remission" (remissione spontanea), and that the cries of miracle reflect the sentiments of simple-minded (menti semplici) people. They complain that Gemma does not return their phone calls or letters, as if this indicates deception on her part. The implication is that Gemma now has pupils and is trying to hide the fact. But if she does have pupils, either they just happened to develop in "spontaneous" fashion as a mere coincidence after the Pio visit, or they became present because of his intercessory prayers. Thus, the existence of pupils would not rule out a possible miracle.

However, it is unlikely that she does have pupils for the following reason: it would mean either that the oculists and other witnesses who failed to detect pupils after the Pio visit were all mistaken, or that she and her family have been lying about the results of the examinations. It is hard to conceive that someone who confessed to Padre Pio (a saint who had the well-documented gift of reading souls) and asked his permission to talk about the incident, would be living a lie. Skepticism is an "attitude" which can at times be healthy, but often replaces an objective search for truth with a persistent attitude of bias that leads to improbable scenarios.

Cicap does report, correctly so, that in 1947 Padre Agostino of the friary at San Giovanni requested specific documentation or testimony that could attest to her condition. But Cicap then incorrectly states that Agostino's request remains unanswered to this day. Padre Agostino, however, wrote in his diary that in February, 1948, he received an affidavit from Dr. Contino, one of the first specialists to examine Gemma when she was still a small child. That report did not mention anything about a lack of pupils, but did say that "...she was not born blind but that her ability to see was uncertain." [24] Contino examined her again after the visit to Padre Pio, and had no doubt that Gemma could now see. Dr. Guglielmo Sanguinetti, the medical director of the hospital founded by Padre Pio, read the Contino affidavit, and speculated that the cure did not exceed "natural powers." [25] However, Sanguinetti never examined Gemma herself.

Bernard Ruffin in his work *Padre Pio: The True Story*, states that in 1979 Fr. Joseph Pius, who was assigned to Pio's friary at that time, wrote that "Gemma has pupils. As a matter of fact, the entire eye is one very large pupil." [26] Gemma's eyes do appear to show large circles of a homogenous dark color, as if it she had very enlarged pupils covering the whole iris. The medical condition of having little or no iris, with extremely large pupils, is called aniridia. If Gemma does in fact have aniridia, it would mean that all of the eye specialists that examined her did not know the difference between an eye with an iris but no pupil vs. an eye with a very large pupil and no iris. While such a mistaken diagnosis is possible, it does not seem likely. At any rate, even a diagnosis of aniridia still leaves the dramatic return of her vision unexplained.

Secondary to the issue of her ability to see, is the question of whether or not she has now developed pupils. The family contends that examinations both before and after the Pio visit showed the absence of pupils. She is in fact officially classified as legally blind.[27] Gemma's case seems to fall in the category of those "ongoing" miracles where the physical symptoms of the malady still exist, but the person functions as if there were nothing amiss. Some of the miraculous cures attributed to Padre Pio's intercession fall into this category. "From a scientific viewpoint, they are still sick." [28] An example of this type of ongoing miracle is the image of Our Lady of Gaudalupe in Mexico, where the Blessed Virgin's image has remained intact on a fiber cloak that should have disintegrated centuries ago.

There is not enough available documentation surrounding this phenomenon to make a truly definitive conclusion. Unlike miracles proposed for Vatican investigation in the "Causes" of beatification or canonization, there is no authoritative testimony that the restoration of Gemma's vision is unexplainable by medical science. However, there is also no concrete evidence to disprove the allegation of "miracle."

Considering this mystery in terms of probabilities – there is a high probability that Gemma was born without pupils and could not see. It is a virtual certainty that she visited Padre Pio, who prayed for her and blessed her eyes. There is a very high probability that she regained her sight during and after visiting the saint, although the physical condition of her eyes remained unchanged. Thus, it seems quite probable that God did in fact work a miracle for Gemma through the intercession of Padre Pio, allowing her to see without pupils, in defiance of the laws of nature.

## Notes

1. Carroll, Malachy Gerard, *Padre Pio*, Chicago, Henry Regnery Company, 1955, p. 55.

2. *Ibid.*, p. 56.

3. Allegri, Renzo, *Padre Pio: Man of Hope*, Ann Arbor, MI, Servant Publications, 2000, p. 180.

4. Cataneo, Pascal, *Padre Pio Gleanings*, Sherbrooke, Quebec, Editions Paulines, 1991, p. 112.

5. www.donatocalabrese.it/padrepio/ritorno.htm, "Il ritorno alla normalita."

6. Allegri, p. 181.

7. Bruno, Clarice, *Roads to Padre Pio*, Barto, PA., National Centre for Padre Pio, 1981, p. 113.

8. Carty, Rev. Charles Mortimer, *Padre Pio: The Stigmatist*, Rockford, IL., Tan Books and Publishers, Inc., 1973, p. 160.

9. Bruno, p. 113.

10. *Ibid.*, p. 114.

11. Allegri, p. 181.

12. *Ibid.*

13. Bruno, p . 115.

14. Allegri, p. 181.

15. *Ibid.*

16. *Ibid.*

17. Winowska, Maria, *The True Face of Padre Pio*, London, The Catholic Book Club, 1961, p. 139.

18. Bruno, p. 112.

19. *Ibid.*, p. 111.

20. Allegri, p. 179.

21. Ruffin, C. Bernard, *Padre Pio: The True*

*Story (Revised and Expanded),* Huntington, IN, Our Sunday Visitor, 1991, p. 333.

22. Maria Calandra, personal communication (email) of November 17, 2004.

23. www.cicap.org/emilia/pupille.htm, "La Donna che vede senza Pupille."

24. Ruffin, p. 333.

25. *Ibid.*, p. 334.

26. *Ibid.*

27. *Ibid.*

28. Allegri, p. 179.

# Chapter Eight

## St. Pio and Pope Paul VI's *Humanae Vitae*

St. Pio defended the controversial encyclical, praising its "lofty teachings" and "eternal truths." An aspect of the document often overlooked today is its grim warning that governments might "impose" contraceptive methods on citizens. In the light of *Humanae Vitae's* other accurate predictions, are mandatory birth control and abortion on the horizon for America?

"...it is never lawful, even for the gravest reasons to do evil that good may come of it – in other words to intend directly something which of its very nature contradicts the moral order, and which must therefore be judged as unworthy of man, even though the intention is to protect or promote the welfare of an individual, of a family, or of society in general. Consequently it is a serious error to think that a whole married life of otherwise normal relations can justify sexual intercourse which is deliberately contraceptive and so intrinsically wrong." Pope Paul VI, *Humanae Vitae.*

St. Padre Pio demonstrated the depth of his love and loyalty to the Church when he publicly praised and defended Pope Paul VI for his encyclical *Humanae Vitae, "Of Human Life."* [1] Upon its release in the summer of 1968, a torrent of vilification and disobedience was unleashed upon the Pontiff from within the Church, as well as mockery and scorn from without. Such open rebellion against Peter's successor was unprecedented, and yet he had done nothing more than his solemn duty to uphold the infallible, magisterial teaching of Catholicism against unnatural methods of birth control.

The likes of Fr. Hans Kung, Fr. Charles Curran, et al, and the Canadian Bishops' Winnipeg Statement, brazenly stood in opposition to the teachings of their own religion. Many did defend the document; but one great saint, a man whom God had raised up as a beacon to guide countless souls during a century of wars and materialism, was conspicuous in his support of the Pope and his encyclical. Only two weeks before his own death in September of that year, St. Padre Pio wrote an inspired and moving letter to the Holy Father which was printed in the Vatican's official newspaper *L'Osservatore Romano*. [2] It is an epistle of great significance, and will likely be part of the evidence put forth in his favor should St. Pio be declared a Doctor of the Church. He is effusive in his praise of the Pope's encyclical, referring to its "lofty teachings," "eternal truths," "clear and decisive words," and its "inspired directives."

In his letter, St. Pio recognizes that the source of the pope's greatest suffering is the disobedience of so many within the Church to his magisterial teachings.

> I know that Your heart suffers much these days on account of the happenings in the

> Church, for peace in the world, for the great needs of its peoples; but above all, for the lack of obedience of some, even Catholics, to the lofty teachings which You, assisted by the Holy Spirit and in the name of God, have given us.

He understands that the Holy Father is carrying his personal cross in Christ's footsteps, following the narrow way of the truth. St. Pio offers his own sufferings and prayers so that the Pope can persevere in his mission.

> I offer Your Holiness my daily prayers and sufferings, the insignificant but sincere offering of the least of your sons, asking the Lord to comfort you with His grace to continue along the direct yet often burdensome way—in defense of those eternal truths which can never change with the times.

He specifically mentions the encyclical and fully supports and obeys what he considers its inspired teaching.

I thank Your Holiness for the clear and decisive words You have spoken in the recent encyclical, *Humanae Vitae*, and I reaffirm my own faith and my unconditional obedience to Your inspired directives.

The reaction against *Humanae Vitae* institutionalized dissent within the Church, and it became fashionable for liberal Catholics to openly disagree with and disobey church teachings that were in conflict with their own personal predilections. It is quite commendable that today many Catholic Bishops are clearly presenting the Church's teaching on life issues, especially in the light of the recent statements by Catholic politicians who attempt to justify their support for pro-abortion legislation. Unfortunately, many liberal Catholics don't particularly care if they disagree with Church teaching. For such as these, stronger medicine is needed, which goes beyond presenting them with the truths of the Faith.

Padre Pio understood this, and administered this powerful medicine in his confessional. Although for the vast majority of penitents he was gracious, cordial, and encouraging, when necessary he had recourse to drastic methods that even today shock those who learn of them. In these extreme cases, when faced with an unrepentant sinner, he would deny them absolution in the Sacrament of Confession. To any who were exceptionally stubborn in their refusal to admit guilt, he would even publicly and vocally chase them out of the confessional. But he only administered these jolts in order to make such people aware that their refusal to accept the truths of the faith, and to live them out, endangered their personal salvation. Padre Pio: "If you only knew what it costs me to refuse absolution! Remember, it is better to be reprimanded by a man in this world, than by God in the next!" [3]

Padre Pio spoke up during elections in Italy after World War II, when there was a strong possibility that the Communist Party would win in the polls. He was known to tell pilgrims to his friary at San Giovanni Rotondo that they should not vote for Communists. In fact, the Communist party blamed Padre Pio for their defeat in two of the general elections held during the late 1940's. [4]

What would Padre Pio have said to those pro-abortion Catholic politicians of today who insist on describing themselves as faithful Catholics? Would he boot the likes of Nancy

Pelosi and Joe Biden out of his confessional, if they insisted on defending their support of pro-abortion legislation? Hopefully, when in the actual presence of the saint, they would be touched by God's grace and realize their mistake. But if they persisted . . . ? Would he speak out against a political party whose official platform supported abortion, and whose presidential candidate was an extremist on the issue, resolutely committed to the support of this intrinsic evil? Would he say that those who vote for such candidates are endangering their own salvation and risking eternal damnation? As St. Pio famously replied to an unrepentant liberal who said he did not believe in hell, "You will when you get there!" [5]

The excuse most commonly offered by Catholic politicians who support and enable legalized abortion, is that they have no right to impose their faith on other members of society. But Pope Paul VI addresses even this issue in his encyclical *Humanae Vitae*. He denotes the priorities and hierarchy of duties which apply to " . . . the objective moral order which was established by God, and of which a right conscience is the true interpreter." Our first duty is to God, then to ourselves and our salvation, to our families, and to society. "In a word, the exercise of responsible parenthood requires that husband and wife, keeping a right order of priorities, recognize their own duties toward God, themselves, their families and human society" (Section #10). The "don't want to impose" politicians are placing what they allege is a duty towards society before their duty to God, showing that they care little for either by their support for this great evil.

## A "right" to abortion might become a "duty"

It is often pointed out that *Humanae Vitae* was quite prophetic in its warning of the general moral decline in society that would result from its adoption of artificial birth control methods. In Section #17 certain specific predictions were made by the Holy Father. "Let them first consider how easily this course of action could open wide the way for marital infidelity and a general lowering of moral standards." Along with infidelity and a lowering of morality, this section of the document makes a third and fourth prediction. The third is that the partner would be considered as nothing more than a mere instrument for the satisfaction of selfish desires.

Since the above three have come to pass in democratic societies, it is well advised to at least try to prevent the fourth from doing so, since it involves the most serious of consequences. This fourth prophetic warning from section #17 is the fear that governments will "impose" mandatory birth control upon their citizens. It is one to which too little attention has been paid, since it is as yet largely unfulfilled with the possible exception of Communist China, although that government denies responsibility for forced abortions in implementing its "one child policy". [6,7]

Although Pope Paul VI in his encyclical formulates this warning while addressing contraception, forty years later it applies even more importantly to abortion. (At the time of *Humanae Vitae* legalized abortion in the West was still five to ten years in the future).

> Finally, careful consideration should be given to the danger of this power passing into the hands of those public authorities who care little for the precepts of the moral law. Who will blame a government which in its attempt to resolve the problems affecting an entire country resorts to the same measures as are

regarded as lawful by married people in the solution of a particular family difficulty? Who will prevent public authorities from favoring those contraceptive methods which they consider more effective? Should they regard this as necessary, they may even impose their use on everyone.

He continues by emphasizing the danger that people ". . . may give into the hands of public authorities the power to intervene in the most personal and intimate responsibility of husband and wife." Essentially, what has started out as a "right" to choose to prevent or terminate a pregnancy, might end up as a "*duty*" to choose to terminate." *Humanae Vitae* is more relevant today than ever.

"The first thing I'd do as president is sign the Freedom of Choice Act," Barack Obama said in a speech to abortion advocates concerned about pro-life protections at the state level.[8] The Freedom of Choice Act (FOCA) [9] is legislation co-sponsored by Barack Obama which would nullify all state laws that in any way attempt to limit or regulate abortion, including partial-birth abortion. It specifies that government will not interfere with a woman's choice to either keep or kill her unborn child. Nevertheless, FOCA would be a major move towards the dangerous precipice of government-mandated abortion, since it would consolidate all power over birth control into the hands of federal law and authorities. From there it would only be a small step to amend it in the light of overriding national health interests, environmental or population concerns, or any other reason deemed appropriate. Thus the FOCA clause in section 4.b.1.a, stating that a woman has the "right to choose to bear a child" could conveniently and easily be changed to, for example, that a woman has the right to choose to bear *up to two children.* More ominously, it could be amended to state that a woman has the right to bear a child, except in cases of rape, incest, Down syndrome, etc.

This is not to imply that any particular individual or group *currently* has an agenda for mandatory abortion, but the potential clearly exists. The growth of the culture of death is not going to stop with the codification of Roe v. Wade by FOCA, but will continue unless it is rooted out completely. Roe v. Wade was one of the early phases in the march along this highway of ruin. FOCA would take us another step closer to the fulfillment of *Humanae Vitae's* prophetic warning of government imposition and intervention in the area of " . . . the most personal and intimate responsibility of husband and wife."

Perhaps the greatest glory of the Catholic Church today is its public stand against the culture of death. Let us pray along with Padre Pio, at the close of his letter to His Holiness, that these "disturbing clouds pass over," and that the onslaught of the abortion juggernaut will be derailed through the efforts of loyal Catholics and others.

> May God grant victory to the truth, peace to his Church, tranquility to the world, health and prosperity to your Holiness so that, once these fleeting doubts are dissipated, the Kingdom of God may triumph in all hearts, guided by your apostolic work as Supreme Pastor of all Christianity.

# Notes

1. Encyclical Letter *Humanae Vitae* of the Supreme Pontiff Paul VI. http://www.vatican.va/holy_father/paul_vi/encyclicals/documents/hf_p-vi_enc_25071968_humanae-vitae_en.html
2. *Una Lettera di Padre Pio, in L'Osservatore Romano, September 29, 1968. http://www.ewtn.com/library/MARY/PIOPOPE.HTM*
3. *Mary F. Ingoldsby,* Padre Pio: His Life and Mission, *(Dublin: Veritas Publications, 1978), p. 68.*
4. *C. Bernard Ruffin,* Padre Pio: The True Story, *(Huntington, IN: Our Sunday Visitor, 1991), p. 272.*
5. *Gherardo Leone,* Padre Pio Teaches Us, *(San Giovanni Rotondo, Italy: La Casa Sollievo Editions, 1974), p. 97.*
6. *Cases of Forced Abortion Surface in China.*http://www.npr.org/templates/story/story.php?storyId=9766870
7. China's One Child Policy.http://geography.about.com/od/populationgeography/a/onechild.htm

8. Obama's Abortion Bombshell: Unrestricted Abortion Over Wishes of Individual States a Priority for Presidency. http://www.lifesitenews.com/ldn/2008/jun/08061010.html
9. Freedom of Choice Act (FOCA). http://www.nrlc.org/FOCA/index.html.

## Appendix to Chapter Eight

## Padre Pio's Letter to Pope Paul VI

Your Holiness,

I unite myself with my brothers and present at your feet my affectionate respect, all my devotion to your august person in an act of faith, love and obedience to the dignity of him whom you are representing on this earth. The Capuchin Order has always been in the first line in love, fidelity, obedience and devotion to the Holy See; I pray to God that it may remain thus and continue in its tradition of religious seriousness and austerity, evangelical poverty and faithful observance of the Rule and

Constitution, certainly renewing itself in the vitality and in the inner spirit, according to the guides of the Second Vatican Council, in order to be always ready to attend to the necessities of Mother Church under the rule of your Holiness.

I know that your heart is suffering much these days in the interest of the Church, for the peace of the world, for the innumerable necessities of the people of the world, but above all, for the lack of obedience of some, even Catholics, to the high teaching that you, assisted by the Holy Spirit and in the name of God, are giving us. I offer you my prayers and daily sufferings as a small but sincere contribution on the part of the least of your sons in order that God may give you comfort with his Grace to follow the straight and painful way in the defense of eternal truth, which never changes with the passing of the years. Also, in the name of my spiritual children and the Prayer Groups, I thank you for your clear and decisive words that you especially pronounced in the last encyclical *Humanae Vitae*; and I reaffirm my faith, my unconditional obedience to your illuminated directions.

May God grant victory to the truth, peace to his Church, tranquility to the world, health and prosperity to your Holiness so that, once these fleeting doubts are dissipated, the Kingdom of God may triumph in all hearts, guided by your apostolic work as Supreme Pastor of all Christianity.

Prostrate at your feet, I beg you to bless me in the company of my brothers in religion, my spiritual children, the Prayer Groups, my sick ones and also to bless all our good endeavours which we are trying to fulfill under your protection in the name of Jesus.

Humbly yours,
P. Pio, Capuchin

Taken from
http://www.ewtn.com/library/MARY/PIOPOPE.HTM

# Chapter Nine

## Padre Pio and the Tale of the Empty Tomb

A strange tale regarding Padre Pio has recently resurfaced – a rumor which, according to an article on the Internet,[1] originally appeared in a Catholic periodical in October 2002.[2] It alleges that a secret exhumation of Padre Pio was ordered by the Vatican in preparation for his May 2, 1999 Beatification ceremony.

According to this article, the top-secret exhumation revealed that the body of the saint was no longer in its coffin! Only his robe, cincture, and sandals were present. Elaborations of the original account claim that, since the tomb was empty in 1999, the body of Padre Pio exposed for veneration in San Giovanni Rotondo in 2008 was actually a double, the body of another man!

There are innumerable problems with the empty tomb tale, not the least of which is the implication that Padre Pio was given celestial honors equal to the Blessed Virgin Mary, and was assumed into heaven. "Assuming" that God would perform this miracle, why keep such a wonder a big secret? In fact, what would be the reason for performing the 1999 exhumation clandestinely in the first place? The article in question offers no explanation.

As will be seen below in the description of the exhumation performed on March 2, 2008, it would have been virtually impossible to conduct such a complex operation covertly in 1999. The crypt area must be closed to pilgrims for a number of days and special equipment brought in, something that would immediately be noticed by the people of San Giovanni Rotondo. The empty tomb story asserts that there was a three-ton block of "Italian marble" over the tomb that had to be moved. However, an item in the official magazine published by Padre Pio's Friary, "The Voice of Padre Pio" (March/April 2008), states that there was in fact a monolithic block of Labrador granite covering the burial space.

The rumor relies on the testimony of three people, interviewed by the writer of the article.

Two of them are members of a family in Connecticut. These two people heard the story from a French priest. This priest was a friend of the late Silvio Cardinal Oddi, who supposedly saw the empty tomb. Although allegedly sworn to secrecy, the Cardinal told the story to the priest. In other words, the testimony of the people from Connecticut is two levels removed from the eyewitness to the purported 1999 exhumation. An aside: the priest's name is given as Chamoine de Porta, a name found nowhere else on an Internet search except in that story.

The other testimony upon which the writer based the story was from the late Capuchin priest, Fr. Carl Pulvermacher: he ". . . has corroborated this story." What does that mean? Did he hear it from the people in Connecticut? Was he a first hand witness? No clarification is given.

In a 2003 article, Michael Brown of www.spiritdaily.com said this about the empty tomb legend: "That has been the wildest rumor, and as far as we can tell, there's no truth to that. We checked through a foundation in Connecticut [The Padre Pio Foundation, www.padrepio.com] devoted to the new saint, and they in turn were in consultation with the

Franciscans who administer his shrine in Italy. From what we understand, the tomb has not even been opened." [3]

The writer of the story also spoke to the late John McCaffery, an author and close friend of Padre Pio. In a conversation with the saint, McCaffery mentioned the millions of pilgrims who would come to visit his tomb after he died. Padre Pio's response, as reported in the article: "John," he said slowly, emphasizing every word, "Let them come! I will not be here!" This is truly an unusual and cryptic remark. But did the Scotch-Irish Mr. McCaffery clearly understand what Padre Pio, who regularly spoke in southern Italian dialect, intended to say in this exchange? The McCaffery anecdote is in contrast to a published account that Padre Pio wanted people to come and visit with him at his tomb after his death:

> ". . . there were many of his spiritual children who asked of the Padre, especially when he was approaching the time of his death: "Now that you may leave us, what are we going to do without you?" He replied, gruffly but at the same time playfully, "Silly person, I will be here in your midst, more than before. Come

visit my tomb. Before, in order to speak to me, you had to wait. Then, it is I who will be waiting there. Come to my tomb and you will receive more than you did before!" [4]

All three of the testimonies cited in the empty tomb account agree that at the time of the exhumation, "Nothing was said, except they closed the coffin and told everyone nothing." In that case, when was a so-called substitute body placed in the coffin? In the item featured in the aforementioned 2008 edition of "The Voice of Padre Pio," there is a photograph of row upon row of the one hundred Capuchins present as witnesses at the real exhumation on March 2, 2008.

Archbishop Mgr. Domenico Umberto D'Ambrosio, the Delegate to the Holy See for the Shrine and Apostolic Works of Padre Pio, supervised the operation. Also present were a host of civil and ecclesiastical authorities, doctors, relations of the saint, and others among the faithful. Included was the Minister General of the Order of the Capuchin Friars Minor, Fr. Mauro Johri. The block of Labrador granite had been removed on a prior day, but there were still four reinforced concrete slabs in place over the coffin on March 2.

On Feb. 28, when the granite block was removed, the members of the ecclesiastical tribunal who were present took an "oath of faith' over the Bible, concerning the procedures that they would witness. Then five people present at the original 1968 burial of the saint took a formal oath that the tomb was in the same condition as they had left it.

Subsequently on March 2, the four concrete slabs protecting the coffin were removed in the presence of scores of onlookers, with the process documented by TV and photographic equipment. A steel plate covering the coffin was also removed. Strong ropes and pulleys had to be employed to raise the coffin to floor level. The Friary's magazine reports that: " . . . the Archbishop who, assisted by the Promoter of Justice and by the Registered Notary, after checking that they were intact, broke the seals that had been made the evening of 26 September 1968." Solderers then were summoned in order to cut the edges of the zinc case.

Following this, the Archbishop and a commission of five medical experts inspected the body, including the medical Director of

Padre Pio's hospital "The Home for the Relief of Suffering," Dr. Luigi Pacilli, and Dr. Michele Bisceglia, representing the Holy See. In the light of this well-documented and highly visible process, how could anyone reasonably assert that somehow another body was surreptitiously placed in "the empty coffin?" Yet there are some who still insist (in private emails that are circulating) that the original empty tomb story is true, and thus they are forced to propose a Padre Pio "double." Are they then implying that some or all of the many high Church officials and respected medical professionals involved in the 2008 exhumation process are perpetrators of a gigantic hoax? The apocryphal tale of the empty tomb of Padre Pio only reinforces a regrettable image of fanaticism surrounding the life, and even the death, of one of the greatest saints in history.

## Notes

1. www.freerepublic.com/focus/f-religion/771264/posts, "St. Padre Pio's Body not Found in his Tomb?"

2. http://www.ourladyofgoodsuccess.com/frames-3-4-2005/padre-pio/the-empty-tomb-2002.pdf, "St. Padre Pio's Body not Found in his Tomb?"

3. http://www.spiritdaily.org/Prophecy-seers/Pioupdate.htm, "A year after his Canonization, Rumors, Miracles and Memories follow St. Pio."

4. http://www.sanpadrepio.com/promise.htm, "The Great Promise of St. Padre Pio."

# Chapter Ten

## The Amazing Story of Giovanna Rizzani

While still a young seminarian of only about 18 years old, Brother Pio was studying in the friary of St. Elia a Pianisi. It was here that he had, as far as is known, his first experience of bilocation. It was so unusual and significant that he wrote down the events that occurred and consigned it to his spiritual advisor, Padre Agostino. The contents of this note have been preserved through the years, and in fact it was presented, along with the rest of this story, as part of the documentation in the process for the Beatification of Padre Pio. It reads as follows:

> Several days ago I had an extraordinary experience. About 11:00 in the evening [of January 18, 1905] Brother Anastasio and I were in the choir. Suddenly I found myself at the same time in the palace of an extremely wealthy family. The master of the house was dying just as his daughter was about to be born.

Then the Blessed Mother appeared and, turning to me, said, "I am entrusting this unborn child to your care and protection. Although she will become a precious jewel, right now she has no form. Shape and polish her. Make her as brilliant as you can, because one day I would like to adorn myself with her."

I replied, "How can this be possible? I am only a poor seminarian and don't even know whether I will have the joy and good fortune to become a priest. Even if I do, how will I ever be able to take care of this girl since I will be so far way from here?"

The Blessed Mother admonished me, "Don't doubt me. She will come to you, but first you will find her in the Basilica of St. Peter's in Rome."

After that I found myself back in the choir.

All of this information and what follows was pieced together in later interviews the Capuchin Fathers held with Padre Pio, the daughter and her mother. [1, 2, 3, 4]

## Giovanna's Birth

As the father of his as yet unborn daughter, Giovanna, lay dying, his pregnant wife was tearfully praying by his bedside. She looked up, and saw the figure of a Capuchin monk leaving the room. She went out after him down the corridor but he had disappeared.

At that moment the family watchdog, which was tied up outside, began to howl mournfully, sensing the approaching death of his master. He wife then went downstairs in order to untie the dog. While still in the house, she suddenly and prematurely gave birth, without pain or complications, to her daughter Giovanna. The priest that had come to administer last rites to her husband thus was also able to immediately baptize her infant.

The master of the house had died peacefully, reconciled with the Church, although just prior to his final illness he had been an unbeliever, refusing to see a priest. During Brother Pio's visit in bilocation he had prayed for the salvation of the man, as the Blessed Virgin had asked him to do.

Giovanna's mother took her and the rest of the family to reside in Rome after her husband's death. Giovanna was destined to be spiritually guided and molded by Padre Pio. But, during her youth, her agnostic school teachers at the high school level created doubts in her mind about the Faith. Although she was a devout Catholic, she became tormented by these doubts, especially about the mystery of the Holy Trinity. She began to look for a holy priest who could enlighten her, but was unsuccessful.

One day in 1922, as a teenager around 17 years old, Giovanna and a girlfriend visited St. Peter's Basilica, hoping to find there a priest that could explain the many questions she had about the Faith. The hour was late, and no priests were to be found. One of the sacristans told them that the Basilica would close in a half hour, and that perhaps she could still find a priest who had not yet left.

The two girls continued their search, and finally saw a priest, a young Capuchin. Giovanna respectfully approached him, asking if he would listen to her to calm her spirit. The Capuchin agreed and he entered the second confessional on the left. Kneeling in the booth, Giovanna explained that she did not actually come for confession, but for an answer to many doubts about the Faith that she had, especially regarding the Most Holy Trinity.

The sympathetic priest began to explain that many mysteries of God can never be fully understood, and they will always remain mysteries. But some can be understood better by way of similes. He than began to compare the Trinity to the way bread is made, from three distinct components, flour, water and leaven. The three are combined into one substance. Then with this dough, three loaves are made, each loaf has the same substance as the others, but they are distinct one from the other. Using similes such as this, the Capuchin, who of course was Padre Pio, was able to clear up the doubts that had been tormenting Giovanna about the Trinity, and other aspects of the Faith.

She left the confessional "radiant with joy." Thus was fulfilled the second part of the prediction made by Our Lady to Padre Pio in long ago 1905, that *"She will come to you, but first you will find her in the Basilica of St. Peter's in Rome."*

Giovanna told her friend that this was such a kind and learned priest, that they should wait here for him to come out of the confessional. Then they could ask him where he was assigned, so that in the future they would be able to receive his advise and go to him for confession.

They waited at the spot, but the Capuchin never exited the confessional. Then the sacristan came by and said that the Basilica was now closing and they would have to leave. They girls explained that they were waiting for the priest to come out so that they could greet him. Concerned that he might lock him inside when the Basilica closed, the sacristan opened the door of the confessional and found it empty. There was no one else around. The girls were bewildered, since they had not moved from the spot and had seen no one leave the confessional. Perturbed and confused, the young ladies went home. This was the second time that Padre Pio had visited Giovanna in bilocation. The first time was when she was still in her mother's womb, just about to be born.

However, she had no suspicion that the priest in the confessional was Padre Pio. This was to change a year later in 1923 when during the summer vacation from college Giovanna, her aunt, and some friends went to the friary in San Giovanni Rotondo to make the acquaintance of the stigmatized friar. The first afternoon, they were waiting with many others for Padre Pio to pass by in the corridor that leads from the sacristy to the cloister. Although the area was packed with people, Giovanna found herself in the front row, and as Padre Pio came by, he held out his pierced, gloved hand for her to kiss, while saying to her: "Giovanna! I know you. You were born the day in which your father died." She was astounded, because it was impossible that Padre Pio could have known this.

The next day she went to Padre Pio for confession, and his first words were, "My daughter, you have finally come! How many years have I waited for you." Giovanna thought he had mistaken her for someone else, since this was the first time she had been to San Giovanni. Then Padre Pio revealed to her that he was the priest that had dispelled her doubts about the Blessed Trinity at St. Peter's in Rome the summer before. He then explained to her the mysterious visit he had made in bilocation to her family's home in Northern Italy the evening she was born, as her father lay dying. He explained that the Blessed Virgin herself had entrusted her to his spiritual care. She had finally come to see him, and now was the time for him to begin to polish and form her soul. Giovanna was so moved with emotion at hearing all this that she burst into tears.

But she did not doubt. She asked him what she must do, become a nun perhaps? Padre replied: "Nothing like that. You will come often to San Giovanni Rotondo, I will have care of your soul, and you will know the will of God."

For the next forty-five years, until Padre's passing in 1968, Giovanna visited him often for spiritual direction, and confessed almost exclusively to him. On one occasion she asked him, "Padre, do you really care for me? He replied: "How could I not care for you. You are the first born of my heart. Love Jesus. Love Our Lady, who thought of you before you were born!"

Giovanna married and had a family, and at the request of Padre Pio became a Third Order Franciscan. The Third Order is primarily for laypersons, married or single, who feel called to respond to the charism of the seraphic St. Francis. Padre Pio told Giovanna, "Here you can draw from and reach the evangelic spirit of the Seraphic Father (Francis). It is my ardent desire that all my spiritual children belong to one of the Franciscan families so that I can truly feel I am their Father and Brother."

At that time, Padre Pio was the spiritual advisor to the Third Order Fraternity that was connected with the Friary at San Giovanni Rotondo. He personally received her into the fraternity, and gave her the Third Order name of Sister Jacopa. Giovanna was quite unhappy with this name, since she wanted her Franciscan name to be Clare. However, Padre Pio explained to her that Lady Jacopa was a noblewoman of Rome who was so close to Francis and gave so much support and encouragement to his new order of Friars Minor, that she was permitted to be at the beside of the saint to assist him as he lay dying. Padre Pio wanted Giovanna to be called Jacopa for a very important reason. He prophesied to her that just as the Roman lady Jacopa was present at the death of St. Francis, so would Giovanna, Sister Jacopa, be present at his own death. And it happened this way, even though Padre Pio died in his own cell within the monastery cloister, and no women were allowed in that area.

## Witness to his Death

Not long before Padre Pio's passing in 1968, Giovanna, who lived in Rome, heard the voice of Padre Pio calling her: "Come immediately to San Giovanni Rotondo, because I am leaving.

If you delay, you will never see me again." Giovanna, who was now quite elderly, immediately set out for the town, accompanied by her very close friend, Margaret Hamilton. A few days before his death, Giovanna was able to confess to the saint, who told her, "This is the last confession you will have with me. Now I give you absolution for all the sins you committed from the age of reason to this moment." He added, "My hour has arrived. Jesus is coming to meet me." Giovanna burst into tears as she exited the confessional.

She and Margaret Hamilton attended Padre Pio's last Mass, held on September 22, 1968. It was a special weekend in honor of the 50 years of his stigmata, and tens of thousands of his spiritual children and prayer groups were in San Giovanni Rotondo for the occasion. She and her friend retired to their room in the nearby *pensione* where they were staying, but Giovanna was restless and unable to sleep. Outside the dogs were howling. Then, in the early hours of the 23rd, Padre Pio passed away. For approximately two hours, from a half-hour after midnight until 2:30 AM, Giovanna was present through a spiritual vision, a type of bilocation, in the very cell of the saint for the last moments of his life. She saw him make his confession to Padre Pellegrino, saw the two of them walk to the veranda for a few minutes, heard Padre Pio renew his religious vows, and saw three doctors enter and try to treat the dying Padre, and heard the last rites administered to him by Padre Paolo.

When the vision was over, she found herself back in the *pensione*. She immediately let out a scream, awakening her friend and insisting that the Padre was very ill and dying, and that she had seen him. "I was in his cell and there were many friars, it was so sad." Margaret tried to tell her was a nightmare but could not calm her. It was 2:30 in the morning, but Giovanna quickly dressed and ran the short distance to the friary. A few minutes later she returned, shouting and screaming, and rousing many in the *pensione*. "The Father is dead, the Father is dead. We are lost persons, we are orphans. We will never have him again!"

Margaret Hamilton then went out herself to the friary, and large numbers of Carabinieri, the state police, were already there by 3:00 AM. They were as yet prohibited from confirming that Padre Pio had died. She kept begging the commander for information, who replied that he was not permitted to say anything, but he said, "Look at me!" And she saw in the darkness that he was weeping copious tears, even onto his uniform.

Several days later, Giovanna spoke to one of the friars, Padre Alberto, about her vision. He refused to believe it because up until that moment, no woman had ever entered the cell of Padre Pio, nor had it ever been photographed. In the words of Padre Alberto, "Giovanna told me that she would describe Padre Pio's cell as she saw it when he was dying. Imagine my wonder when she proceeded to describe his cell and everything in it to the smallest detail. I could not keep from exclaiming, "Enough! I believe that you were present in his cell when he died!"

## Notes

1. "Itineraries in the Gargano Sant'Elia a Pianisi (Campobasso), "http://www.vocedipadrepio.com/eng/santelia.php.
2. D'Apolito, Padre Alberto, *Padre Pio of Pietrelcina,* San Giovanni Rotondo, Italy, Our Lady of Grace Friary, 1986, Chapter XIV.
3. D'Apolito, Padre Alberto, "Protected by P. Pio all of her life," *The Voice of Padre Pio,*" Volume III, no. 1, 1973, pp. 7-9.
4. Schug, Fr. John A., *A Padre Pio Profile,* Petersham MA., St. Bede's Publications, 1987, Chapter 4.

The above book by Fr. John A. Schug, *A Padre Pio Profile*, is now published by:

The National Centre for Padre Pio, Inc.
P. O. Box 206 (Mailing Address)
111 Barto Road (Visitors Centre)
Barto, PA 19504
Tel: 610-845-3000
www.padrepio.org

# ABOUT THE AUTHOR

Frank Rega is a Third Order Franciscan, and the author of a number of Catholic books, including *Padre Pio and America*, and *St. Francis of Assisi and the Conversion of the Muslims*, both published by TAN Books. He also authored *The Greatest Catholic President, Garcia Moreno of Ecuador*, published by Angelus Press, and a multi-volume series on the *Life of the Mystic Luisa Piccarreta, Journeys in the Divine Will*, published by CreateSpace.

His web page is www.frankrega.com, and email address is regaf@aya.yale.edu.

Made in the USA
Middletown, DE
12 August 2019